THIS BOOK IS

_____

Runner's Log
Complete Daily Training Diary
Sebastian Elliott

There are a lot of web sites and apps for runners. Living in a multiple FitBit household, I know this all too well. These computerized options are great, but they lack the tangibility of a book such as this. Nothing can replace the excitement and pride of holding a completed, physical runner's log book in your hands.

It might be a bit tattered and worse for wear, but you can wrap your hands around it and feel the weight knowing that it represents hours of the joys and pains of your running life. You can flip through it and see your own handwriting reminding you of your commitment and your accomplishments.

I take full advantage of computerized measurement and analysis, but I also keep a physical log and suggest that you do, too. It's a very personal and positive experience that mirrors the personal and positive experience you have when running. *Sebastian*

Copyright © 2015 FastForward Publishing All rights reserved.
Permission to reproduce or transmit in any form or by any means,
electronic or mechanical, including photocopying and recording,
or by any information storage or retrieval system, must be obtained
in writing from FastForward Publishing.

FastForwardPublishing.com

ISBN-13: 978-1507734704
ISBN-10: 1507734700

Table of Contents

Introduction   3

Running Logs   6

Week 1	6	Week 2	10
Week 3	14	Week 4	18
Week 5	22	Week 6	26
Week 7	30	Week 8	34
Week 9	38	Week 10	42
Week 11	46	Week 12	50
Week 13	54	Week 14	58
Week 15	62	Week 16	66
Week 17	70	Week 18	74
Week 19	78	Week 20	82
Week 21	86	Week 22	90
Week 23	94	Week 24	98
Week 25	102	Week 26	106
Week 27	110	Week 28	114
Week 29	118	Week 30	122
Week 31	126	Week 32	130
Week 33	134	Week 34	138
Week 35	142	Week 36	146
Week 37	150	Week 38	154
Week 39	158	Week 40	162
Week 41	166	Week 42	170
Week 43	174	Week 44	178
Week 45	182	Week 46	186
Week 47	190	Week 48	194
Week 49	198	Week 50	202
Week 51	206	Week 52	210

Racing Logs   214

Footwear Log   240

The Perceptive Runner   242

Recommendations   243

Introduction

*"Running has given me the courage to start,
the determination to keep trying, and
the childlike spirit to have fun along the way.
Run often and run long, but
never outrun your joy of running."*

Julie Isphording

One of the most important activities a runner can do is keep a log. Why? Here are 12 quick reasons -- and with a little thought you might come up with half-a-dozen more!

1. **Satisfaction.** When you record a run, it reinforces what you have accomplished.

2. **Motivation.** Running is hard work and it's tough to maintain a high level of motivation. Reviewing your training diary reinforces the investment you have made in the journey to reach your goals.

3. **Pride.** Unlike other activities like painting or woodworking, when you are a runner, you can't see or touch our accomplishments. By recording your runs, all that mileage and achievement is at your fingertips and easy to relive.

4. **Enhanced Performance.** By taking a look at your training log, you can see the cause and effect of your runs over time. Should you increase or decrease your mileage? Do you need more or less speed work. By looking at your workouts over time, you can find ways to train more effectively.

5. **New Shoes.** You should be changing shoes every 300-400 miles. Your log shows you when replacements are in order.

6. **Fixes.** If you have a bad race or an injury, the information in your log can show you how to fix it. Perhaps you have better race performance when the week prior to the race follows a particular pattern or maybe you discover that you tend to get injured in specific circumstances (e.g., increasing weekly mileage above a certain percentage or doing too many miles on hills).

7. **Confidence.** After keeping a running log for a while, flip through the pages you have filled out and see how much hard work you have completed, what you have accomplished and how you've progressed.

8. **Communication.** Share your running diary with a friend, running partner or coach for feedback and or motivation.

9. **Accountability.** A review of your running log reminds you of the standards you have set for yourself as a runner and encourages you to live up to those standards.

10. **Racing.** Log your race results and then compare them to similar races. Also compare those results to your pre-race training. By measuring and comparing race information you will know if you are improving, stalled, or slowing down and make decisions on moving forward to the next race.

11. **Answers.** If you find yourself particularly tired, you can check back in your diary and see if you have had a big jump in mileage or if you have been steadily increasing for too long or find possible answers to a number of different important questions.

12. **Self-Awareness.** Because you are unique, you won't necessarily respond exactly the same was as another runner to a particular training program. Reviewing the data in your log will help you tailor a program that is fine-tuned to you.

Running isn't a sport for pretty boys...
It's about the sweat in your hair and the blisters on your feet.
Its the frozen spit on your chin and the nausea in your gut.
It's about throbbing calves and cramps at midnight that
are strong enough to wake the dead.
It's about getting out the door and running
when the rest of the world is only dreaming about
having the passion that you need to
live each and every day with.
It's about being on a lonely road and running like
a champion even when there's not a single soul
in sight to cheer you on.
Running is all about having the desire to train and
persevere until every fiber in your legs, mind,
and heart is turned to steel.
And when you've finally forged hard enough,
you will have become the best runner you can be.
And that's all that you can ask for.

Paul Maurer

Week of ___/___/_____ - ___/___/_____

Goals for Week: _____

_____

_____

MONDAY	Time	Distance	Pace	Weekly Total
Time of Day	Weather	Route/Course:		
Cross Training:				
How I Felt:				

TUESDAY	Time	Distance	Pace	Weekly Total
Time of Day	Weather	Route/Course:		
Cross Training:				
How I Felt:				

WEDNESDAY	Time	Distance	Pace	Weekly Total
Time of Day	Weather	Route/Course:		
Cross Training:				
How I Felt:				

THURSDAY	Time	Distance	Pace	Weekly Total

Time of Day	Weather	Route/Course:

Cross Training:

How I Felt:

FRIDAY	Time	Distance	Pace	Weekly Total

Time of Day	Weather	Route/Course:

Cross Training:

How I Felt:

SATURDAY	Time	Distance	Pace	Weekly Total

Time of Day	Weather	Route/Course:

Cross Training:

How I Felt:

SUNDAY	Time	Distance	Pace	Weekly Total

Time of Day	Weather	Route/Course:

Cross Training:

How I Felt:

Week 1 Wrap Up

WEEKLY SUMMARY						
Week Total:		Longest Run:			Shortest Run:	
Average:		Monthly Total:			Yearly Total:	
Daily Weight						
Mon	Tues	Wed	Thurs	Fri	sat	Sun
Morning Pulse						
Mon	Tues	Wed	Thurs	Fri	sat	Sun

Did I meet my goals for the week?   ☐ Yes   ☐ No

What helped me reach my goals or what kept me from reaching my goals:

_____

_____

How do I feel about that? _____

_____

What will I change next week? _____

What will I not change next week? _____

Notes/Other Observations: _____

_____

_____

_____

_____

> *"I run because it's so symbolic of life. You have to drive yourself to overcome the obstacles. You might feel that you can't. But then you find your inner strength, and realize you're capable of so much more than you thought."*
>
> **Arthur Blank**

Week of ___/___/_____ - ___/___/_____

Goals for Week: _____

_____

_____

MONDAY	Time	Distance	Pace	Weekly Total
Time of Day	Weather	Route/Course:		
Cross Training:				
How I Felt:				

TUESDAY	Time	Distance	Pace	Weekly Total
Time of Day	Weather	Route/Course:		
Cross Training:				
How I Felt:				

WEDNESDAY	Time	Distance	Pace	Weekly Total
Time of Day	Weather	Route/Course:		
Cross Training:				
How I Felt:				

THURSDAY	Time	Distance	Pace	Weekly Total

Time of Day	Weather	Route/Course:		

Cross Training:
How I Felt:

FRIDAY	Time	Distance	Pace	Weekly Total

Time of Day	Weather	Route/Course:		

Cross Training:
How I Felt:

SATURDAY	Time	Distance	Pace	Weekly Total

Time of Day	Weather	Route/Course:		

Cross Training:
How I Felt:

SUNDAY	Time	Distance	Pace	Weekly Total

Time of Day	Weather	Route/Course:		

Cross Training:
How I Felt:

Week 2 Wrap Up

WEEKLY SUMMARY						
Week Total:			Longest Run:		Shortest Run:	
Average:			Monthly Total:		Yearly Total:	
Daily Weight						
Mon	Tues	Wed	Thurs	Fri	sat	Sun
Morning Pulse						
Mon	Tues	Wed	Thurs	Fri	sat	Sun

Did I meet my goals for the week?   ☐ Yes   ☐ No

What helped me reach my goals or what kept me from reaching my goals:

_____

_____

How do I feel about that? _____

_____

What will I change next week? _____

What will I not change next week? _____

Notes/Other Observations: _____

_____

_____

_____

_____

_____

> *"Occasionally pick up speed-for 2 minutes, tops – then settle back into your former pace. Sometimes this is all you need to snap out of a mental and physical funk. Pick a downhill stretch if you can, and really lengthen your stride."*
>
> **Mark Plaatjes**

Week of ___/___/_____ - ___/___/_____

Goals for Week: _____

_____

_____

MONDAY	Time	Distance	Pace	Weekly Total
Time of Day	Weather	Route/Course:		
Cross Training:				
How I Felt:				

TUESDAY	Time	Distance	Pace	Weekly Total
Time of Day	Weather	Route/Course:		
Cross Training:				
How I Felt:				

WEDNESDAY	Time	Distance	Pace	Weekly Total
Time of Day	Weather	Route/Course:		
Cross Training:				
How I Felt:				

	Time	Distance	Pace	Weekly Total
THURSDAY				

Time of Day	Weather	Route/Course:
Cross Training:		
How I Felt:		

	Time	Distance	Pace	Weekly Total
FRIDAY				

Time of Day	Weather	Route/Course:
Cross Training:		
How I Felt:		

	Time	Distance	Pace	Weekly Total
SATURDAY				

Time of Day	Weather	Route/Course:
Cross Training:		
How I Felt:		

	Time	Distance	Pace	Weekly Total
SUNDAY				

Time of Day	Weather	Route/Course:
Cross Training:		
How I Felt:		

Week 3 Wrap Up

WEEKLY SUMMARY						
Week Total:		Longest Run:			Shortest Run:	
Average:		Monthly Total:			Yearly Total:	
Daily Weight						
Mon	Tues	Wed	Thurs	Fri	sat	Sun
Morning Pulse						
Mon	Tues	Wed	Thurs	Fri	sat	Sun

Did I meet my goals for the week?   ☐ Yes   ☐ No

What helped me reach my goals or what kept me from reaching my goals:

_____

_____

How do I feel about that? _____

_____

What will I change next week? _____

What will I not change next week? _____

Notes/Other Observations: _____

_____

_____

_____

_____

_____

> *"The primary reason to have a coach is to have someone who says: 'Hey, you're looking good today!'"*
>
> **Jack Daniels, Ph.D.**

Week of ___/___/_____ - ___/___/_____

Goals for Week: _____

_____

_____

MONDAY	Time	Distance	Pace	Weekly Total
Time of Day	Weather	Route/Course:		
Cross Training:				
How I Felt:				

TUESDAY	Time	Distance	Pace	Weekly Total
Time of Day	Weather	Route/Course:		
Cross Training:				
How I Felt:				

WEDNESDAY	Time	Distance	Pace	Weekly Total
Time of Day	Weather	Route/Course:		
Cross Training:				
How I Felt:				

THURSDAY	Time	Distance	Pace	Weekly Total

Time of Day	Weather	Route/Course:

Cross Training:
How I Felt:

FRIDAY	Time	Distance	Pace	Weekly Total

Time of Day	Weather	Route/Course:

Cross Training:
How I Felt:

SATURDAY	Time	Distance	Pace	Weekly Total

Time of Day	Weather	Route/Course:

Cross Training:
How I Felt:

SUNDAY	Time	Distance	Pace	Weekly Total

Time of Day	Weather	Route/Course:

Cross Training:
How I Felt:

Week 4 Wrap Up

WEEKLY SUMMARY						
Week Total:		Longest Run:			Shortest Run:	
Average:		Monthly Total:			Yearly Total:	
Daily Weight						
Mon	Tues	Wed	Thurs	Fri	sat	Sun
Morning Pulse						
Mon	Tues	Wed	Thurs	Fri	sat	Sun

Did I meet my goals for the week?   ☐ Yes   ☐ No

What helped me reach my goals or what kept me from reaching my goals:

_____

_____

How do I feel about that? _____

_____

What will I change next week? _____

What will I not change next week? _____

Notes/Other Observations: _____

_____

_____

_____

_____

> *"Somebody may beat me, but they are going to have to bleed to do it."*
>
> **Steve Prefontaine**

Week of ___/___/_____ - ___/___/_____

Goals for Week: _____

_____

_____

	Time	Distance	Pace	Weekly Total
MONDAY				|';

Time of Day	Weather	Route/Course:

Cross Training:
How I Felt:

	Time	Distance	Pace	Weekly Total
TUESDAY				

Time of Day	Weather	Route/Course:

Cross Training:
How I Felt:

	Time	Distance	Pace	Weekly Total
WEDNESDAY				

Time of Day	Weather	Route/Course:

Cross Training:
How I Felt:

THURSDAY	Time	Distance	Pace	Weekly Total

Time of Day	Weather	Route/Course:

Cross Training:

How I Felt:

FRIDAY	Time	Distance	Pace	Weekly Total

Time of Day	Weather	Route/Course:

Cross Training:

How I Felt:

SATURDAY	Time	Distance	Pace	Weekly Total

Time of Day	Weather	Route/Course:

Cross Training:

How I Felt:

SUNDAY	Time	Distance	Pace	Weekly Total

Time of Day	Weather	Route/Course:

Cross Training:

How I Felt:

Week 5 Wrap Up

WEEKLY SUMMARY								
Week Total:			Longest Run:				Shortest Run:	
Average:			Monthly Total:				Yearly Total:	
Daily Weight								
Mon	Tues		Wed	Thurs		Fri	sat	Sun
Morning Pulse								
Mon	Tues		Wed	Thurs		Fri	sat	Sun

Did I meet my goals for the week?   ☐ Yes   ☐ No

What helped me reach my goals or what kept me from reaching my goals:

_____

_____

How do I feel about that? _____

_____

What will I change next week? _____

What will I not change next week? _____

Notes/Other Observations: _____

_____

_____

_____

_____

_____

"Fartlek training ["Fartlek" is Swedish for variable-paced, up-tempo running] can help you build strength and endurance, learn race pace, and practice race tactics all in a single workout."

Bill Dellinger

Week of ___/___/_____ - ___/___/_____

Goals for Week: _____

_____

_____

MONDAY	Time	Distance	Pace	Weekly Total
Time of Day	Weather	Route/Course:		
Cross Training:				
How I Felt:				

TUESDAY	Time	Distance	Pace	Weekly Total
Time of Day	Weather	Route/Course:		
Cross Training:				
How I Felt:				

WEDNESDAY	Time	Distance	Pace	Weekly Total
Time of Day	Weather	Route/Course:		
Cross Training:				
How I Felt:				

THURSDAY	Time	Distance	Pace	Weekly Total

Time of Day	Weather	Route/Course:

Cross Training:
How I Felt:

FRIDAY	Time	Distance	Pace	Weekly Total

Time of Day	Weather	Route/Course:

Cross Training:
How I Felt:

SATURDAY	Time	Distance	Pace	Weekly Total

Time of Day	Weather	Route/Course:

Cross Training:
How I Felt:

SUNDAY	TIme	Distance	Pace	Weekly Total

Time of Day	Weather	Route/Course:

Cross Training:
How I Felt:

Week 6 Wrap Up

WEEKLY SUMMARY						
Week Total:		Longest Run:			Shortest Run:	
Average:		Monthly Total:			Yearly Total:	
Daily Weight						
Mon	Tues	Wed	Thurs	Fri	sat	Sun
Morning Pulse						
Mon	Tues	Wed	Thurs	Fri	sat	Sun

Did I meet my goals for the week?   ☐ Yes   ☐ No

What helped me reach my goals or what kept me from reaching my goals:

_____

_____

How do I feel about that? _____

_____

What will I change next week? _____

What will I not change next week? _____

Notes/Other Observations: _____

_____

_____

_____

_____

_____

"If one can stick to training throughout many long years, then willpower is no longer a problem. It's raining? That doesn't matter. I'm tired? That's beside the point. It's simply that I have to."

Emil Zatopek

Week of ___/___/_____ - ___/___/_____

Goals for Week: _____

_____

_____

MONDAY	Time	Distance	Pace	Weekly Total
Time of Day	Weather	Route/Course:		
Cross Training:				
How I Felt:				

TUESDAY	Time	Distance	Pace	Weekly Total
Time of Day	Weather	Route/Course:		
Cross Training:				
How I Felt:				

WEDNESDAY	Time	Distance	Pace	Weekly Total
Time of Day	Weather	Route/Course:		
Cross Training:				
How I Felt:				

THURSDAY	Time	Distance	Pace	Weekly Total

Time of Day	Weather	Route/Course:

Cross Training:

How I Felt:

FRIDAY	Time	Distance	Pace	Weekly Total

Time of Day	Weather	Route/Course:

Cross Training:

How I Felt:

SATURDAY	Time	Distance	Pace	Weekly Total

Time of Day	Weather	Route/Course:

Cross Training:

How I Felt:

SUNDAY	Time	Distance	Pace	Weekly Total

Time of Day	Weather	Route/Course:

Cross Training:

How I Felt:

Week 7 Wrap Up

WEEKLY SUMMARY						
Week Total:		Longest Run:			Shortest Run:	
Average:		Monthly Total:			Yearly Total:	
Daily Weight						
Mon	Tues	Wed	Thurs	Fri	sat	Sun
Morning Pulse						
Mon	Tues	Wed	Thurs	Fri	sat	Sun

Did I meet my goals for the week?   ☐ Yes   ☐ No

What helped me reach my goals or what kept me from reaching my goals:

_____

_____

How do I feel about that? _____

_____

What will I change next week? _____

What will I not change next week? _____

Notes/Other Observations: _____

_____

_____

_____

_____

> *"Keep working on mental attitude. You have to fight that supposedly rational voice that says: 'I'm 50 years old, and I don't have to be doing this anymore.'"*
>
> **Ken Sparks, Ph.D.**

Week of ___/___/_____ - ___/___/_____

Goals for Week: _____

_____

_____

MONDAY	Time	Distance	Pace	Weekly Total
Time of Day	Weather	Route/Course:		
Cross Training:				
How I Felt:				

TUESDAY	Time	Distance	Pace	Weekly Total
Time of Day	Weather	Route/Course:		
Cross Training:				
How I Felt:				

WEDNESDAY	Time	Distance	Pace	Weekly Total
Time of Day	Weather	Route/Course:		
Cross Training:				
How I Felt:				

THURSDAY	Time	Distance	Pace	Weekly Total
Time of Day	Weather	Route/Course:		
Cross Training:				
How I Felt:				

FRIDAY	Time	Distance	Pace	Weekly Total
Time of Day	Weather	Route/Course:		
Cross Training:				
How I Felt:				

SATURDAY	Time	Distance	Pace	Weekly Total
Time of Day	Weather	Route/Course:		
Cross Training:				
How I Felt:				

SUNDAY	Time	Distance	Pace	Weekly Total
Time of Day	Weather	Route/Course:		
Cross Training:				
How I Felt:				

Week 8 Wrap Up

WEEKLY SUMMARY		
Week Total:	Longest Run:	Shortest Run:
Average:	Monthly Total:	Yearly Total:

Daily Weight						
Mon	Tues	Wed	Thurs	Fri	sat	Sun

Morning Pulse						
Mon	Tues	Wed	Thurs	Fri	sat	Sun

Did I meet my goals for the week? ☐ Yes   ☐ No

What helped me reach my goals or what kept me from reaching my goals:

_____

_____

How do I feel about that? _____

_____

What will I change next week? _____

What will I not change next week? _____

Notes/Other Observations: _____

_____

_____

_____

_____

"Hydrate. Hydrate. Hydrate! In cold weather and warm. We use water to sweat, lubricate joints, tendons, and ligaments, and to carry blood efficiently to major organs. I work all day at hydrating."

Dr. Alex Ratelle

Week of ___/___/_____ - ___/___/_____

Goals for Week: _____

_____

_____

MONDAY	Time	Distance	Pace	Weekly Total
Time of Day	Weather	Route/Course:		
Cross Training:				
How I Felt:				

TUESDAY	Time	Distance	Pace	Weekly Total
Time of Day	Weather	Route/Course:		
Cross Training:				
How I Felt:				

WEDNESDAY	Time	Distance	Pace	Weekly Total
Time of Day	Weather	Route/Course:		
Cross Training:				
How I Felt:				

	Time	Distance	Pace	Weekly Total
THURSDAY				

Time of Day	Weather	Route/Course:
Cross Training:		
How I Felt:		

	Time	Distance	Pace	Weekly Total
FRIDAY				

Time of Day	Weather	Route/Course:
Cross Training:		
How I Felt:		

	Time	Distance	Pace	Weekly Total
SATURDAY				

Time of Day	Weather	Route/Course:
Cross Training:		
How I Felt:		

	Time	Distance	Pace	Weekly Total
SUNDAY				

Time of Day	Weather	Route/Course:
Cross Training:		
How I Felt:		

Week 9 Wrap Up

WEEKLY SUMMARY			
Week Total:	Longest Run:		Shortest Run:
Average:	Monthly Total:		Yearly Total:
Daily Weight			
Mon	Tues	Wed	Thurs	Fri	sat	Sun
Morning Pulse			
Mon	Tues	Wed	Thurs	Fri	sat	Sun

Did I meet my goals for the week?   ☐ Yes   ☐ No

What helped me reach my goals or what kept me from reaching my goals:

_____

_____

How do I feel about that? _____

_____

What will I change next week? _____

What will I not change next week? _____

Notes/Other Observations: _____

_____

_____

_____

_____

_____

> *"I believe in using races as motivators. It's hard to keep on an exercise program if you don't have a significant goal in sight."*
>
> **Bob Greene**

Week of ___/___/_____ - ___/___/_____

Goals for Week: _____

_____

_____

	Time	Distance	Pace	Weekly Total
MONDAY				
Time of Day	Weather	Route/Course:		
Cross Training:				
How I Felt:				

	Time	Distance	Pace	Weekly Total
TUESDAY				
Time of Day	Weather	Route/Course:		
Cross Training:				
How I Felt:				

	Time	Distance	Pace	Weekly Total
WEDNESDAY				
Time of Day	Weather	Route/Course:		
Cross Training:				
How I Felt:				

THURSDAY	Time	Distance	Pace	Weekly Total
Time of Day	Weather	Route/Course:		
Cross Training:				
How I Felt:				

FRIDAY	Time	Distance	Pace	Weekly Total
Time of Day	Weather	Route/Course:		
Cross Training:				
How I Felt:				

SATURDAY	Time	Distance	Pace	Weekly Total
Time of Day	Weather	Route/Course:		
Cross Training:				
How I Felt:				

SUNDAY	Time	Distance	Pace	Weekly Total
Time of Day	Weather	Route/Course:		
Cross Training:				
How I Felt:				

Week 10 Wrap Up

WEEKLY SUMMARY							
Week Total:		Longest Run:			Shortest Run:		
Average:		Monthly Total:			Yearly Total:		
Daily Weight							
Mon	Tues	Wed	Thurs	Fri	sat	Sun	
Morning Pulse							
Mon	Tues	Wed	Thurs	Fri	sat	Sun	

Did I meet my goals for the week?   ☐ Yes   ☐ No

What helped me reach my goals or what kept me from reaching my goals:

_____

_____

How do I feel about that? _____

_____

What will I change next week? _____

What will I not change next week? _____

Notes/Other Observations: _____

_____

_____

_____

_____

> *"If you put down a good solid foundation, you can then build one room after another and pretty soon you have a house. After your base mileage, add hills, pace work, speedwork, and finally race strategy."*
>
> **Rod Dixon**

Week of ___/___/_____ - ___/___/_____

Goals for Week: _____

_____

_____

MONDAY	Time	Distance	Pace	Weekly Total
Time of Day	Weather	Route/Course:		
Cross Training:				
How I Felt:				

TUESDAY	Time	Distance	Pace	Weekly Total
Time of Day	Weather	Route/Course:		
Cross Training:				
How I Felt:				

WEDNESDAY	Time	Distance	Pace	Weekly Total
Time of Day	Weather	Route/Course:		
Cross Training:				
How I Felt:				

THURSDAY	Time	Distance	Pace	Weekly Total
Time of Day	Weather	Route/Course:		
Cross Training:				
How I Felt:				

FRIDAY	Time	Distance	Pace	Weekly Total
Time of Day	Weather	Route/Course:		
Cross Training:				
How I Felt:				

SATURDAY	Time	Distance	Pace	Weekly Total
Time of Day	Weather	Route/Course:		
Cross Training:				
How I Felt:				

SUNDAY	Time	Distance	Pace	Weekly Total
Time of Day	Weather	Route/Course:		
Cross Training:				
How I Felt:				

Week 11 Wrap Up

WEEKLY SUMMARY						
Week Total:		Longest Run:			Shortest Run:	
Average:		Monthly Total:			Yearly Total:	
Daily Weight						
Mon	Tues	Wed	Thurs	Fri	sat	Sun
Morning Pulse						
Mon	Tues	Wed	Thurs	Fri	sat	Sun

Did I meet my goals for the week?   ☐ Yes   ☐ No

What helped me reach my goals or what kept me from reaching my goals:

_____

_____

How do I feel about that? _____

_____

What will I change next week? _____

What will I not change next week? _____

Notes/Other Observations: _____

_____

_____

_____

_____

"Day to day consistency is more important than big mileage. Then you're never shot the next day."

John Campbell

Week of ___/___/_____ - ___/___/_____

Goals for Week: _____

_____

_____

MONDAY	Time	Distance	Pace	Weekly Total
Time of Day	Weather	Route/Course:		
Cross Training:				
How I Felt:				

TUESDAY	Time	Distance	Pace	Weekly Total
Time of Day	Weather	Route/Course:		
Cross Training:				
How I Felt:				

WEDNESDAY	Time	Distance	Pace	Weekly Total
Time of Day	Weather	Route/Course:		
Cross Training:				
How I Felt:				

THURSDAY	Time	Distance	Pace	Weekly Total

Time of Day	Weather	Route/Course:

Cross Training:
How I Felt:

FRIDAY	Time	Distance	Pace	Weekly Total

Time of Day	Weather	Route/Course:

Cross Training:
How I Felt:

SATURDAY	Time	Distance	Pace	Weekly Total

Time of Day	Weather	Route/Course:

Cross Training:
How I Felt:

SUNDAY	Time	Distance	Pace	Weekly Total

Time of Day	Weather	Route/Course:

Cross Training:
How I Felt:

Week 12 Wrap Up

WEEKLY SUMMARY		
Week Total:	Longest Run:	Shortest Run:
Average:	Monthly Total:	Yearly Total:

Daily Weight						
Mon	Tues	Wed	Thurs	Fri	sat	Sun

Morning Pulse						
Mon	Tues	Wed	Thurs	Fri	sat	Sun

Did I meet my goals for the week? ☐ Yes   ☐ No

What helped me reach my goals or what kept me from reaching my goals:

_____

_____

How do I feel about that? _____

_____

What will I change next week? _____

What will I not change next week? _____

Notes/Other Observations: _____

_____

_____

_____

_____

_____

"There are clubs you can't belong to, neighborhoods you can't live in, schools you can't get into, but the roads are always open."

Nike commercial

Week of ___/___/_____ - ___/___/_____

Goals for Week: _____

_____

_____

MONDAY	Time	Distance	Pace	Weekly Total
Time of Day	Weather	Route/Course:		
Cross Training:				
How I Felt:				

TUESDAY	Time	Distance	Pace	Weekly Total
Time of Day	Weather	Route/Course:		
Cross Training:				
How I Felt:				

WEDNESDAY	Time	Distance	Pace	Weekly Total
Time of Day	Weather	Route/Course:		
Cross Training:				
How I Felt:				

THURSDAY	Time	Distance	Pace	Weekly Total

Time of Day	Weather	Route/Course:

Cross Training:

How I Felt:

FRIDAY	Time	Distance	Pace	Weekly Total

Time of Day	Weather	Route/Course:

Cross Training:

How I Felt:

SATURDAY	Time	Distance	Pace	Weekly Total

Time of Day	Weather	Route/Course:

Cross Training:

How I Felt:

SUNDAY	Time	Distance	Pace	Weekly Total

Time of Day	Weather	Route/Course:

Cross Training:

How I Felt:

Week 13 Wrap Up

WEEKLY SUMMARY							
Week Total:		Longest Run:			Shortest Run:		
Average:		Monthly Total:			Yearly Total:		
Daily Weight							
Mon	Tues	Wed	Thurs	Fri	sat	Sun	
Morning Pulse							
Mon	Tues	Wed	Thurs	Fri	sat	Sun	

Did I meet my goals for the week?   ☐ Yes   ☐ No

What helped me reach my goals or what kept me from reaching my goals:

_____

_____

How do I feel about that? _____

_____

What will I change next week? _____

What will I not change next week? _____

Notes/Other Observations: _____

_____

_____

_____

_____

_____

> *"To keep from decaying, to be a winner, the athlete must accept pain - not only accept it, but look for it, live with it, learn not to fear it."*
>
> **George Sheehan**

Week of ___/___/_____ - ___/___/_____

Goals for Week: _____

_____

_____

MONDAY	Time	Distance	Pace	Weekly Total
Time of Day	Weather	Route/Course:		
Cross Training:				
How I Felt:				

TUESDAY	Time	Distance	Pace	Weekly Total
Time of Day	Weather	Route/Course:		
Cross Training:				
How I Felt:				

WEDNESDAY	Time	Distance	Pace	Weekly Total
Time of Day	Weather	Route/Course:		
Cross Training:				
How I Felt:				

THURSDAY	Time	Distance	Pace	Weekly Total

Time of Day	Weather	Route/Course:

Cross Training:

How I Felt:

FRIDAY	Time	Distance	Pace	Weekly Total

Time of Day	Weather	Route/Course:

Cross Training:

How I Felt:

SATURDAY	Time	Distance	Pace	Weekly Total

Time of Day	Weather	Route/Course:

Cross Training:

How I Felt:

SUNDAY	Time	Distance	Pace	Weekly Total

Time of Day	Weather	Route/Course:

Cross Training:

How I Felt:

Week 14 Wrap Up

WEEKLY SUMMARY						
Week Total:		Longest Run:			Shortest Run:	
Average:		Monthly Total:			Yearly Total:	
Daily Weight						
Mon	Tues	Wed	Thurs	Fri	sat	Sun
Morning Pulse						
Mon	Tues	Wed	Thurs	Fri	sat	Sun

Did I meet my goals for the week?   ☐ Yes   ☐ No

What helped me reach my goals or what kept me from reaching my goals:

_____

_____

How do I feel about that? _____

_____

What will I change next week? _____

What will I not change next week? _____

Notes/Other Observations: _____

_____

_____

_____

_____

_____

> *"During long, slow distance training, you should think of yourself as a thoroughbred disguised as a plow horse. No need to give yourself away by running fast."*
>
> **Marty Liquori**

Week of ___/___/_____ - ___/___/_____

Goals for Week: _____

_____

_____

MONDAY	Time	Distance	Pace	Weekly Total
Time of Day	Weather	Route/Course:		
Cross Training:				
How I Felt:				

TUESDAY	Time	Distance	Pace	Weekly Total
Time of Day	Weather	Route/Course:		
Cross Training:				
How I Felt:				

WEDNESDAY	Time	Distance	Pace	Weekly Total
Time of Day	Weather	Route/Course:		
Cross Training:				
How I Felt:				

	Time	Distance	Pace	Weekly Total
THURSDAY				

Time of Day	Weather	Route/Course:
Cross Training:			
How I Felt:			

	Time	Distance	Pace	Weekly Total
FRIDAY				

Time of Day	Weather	Route/Course:
Cross Training:			
How I Felt:			

	Time	Distance	Pace	Weekly Total
SATURDAY				

Time of Day	Weather	Route/Course:
Cross Training:			
How I Felt:			

	Time	Distance	Pace	Weekly Total
SUNDAY				

Time of Day	Weather	Route/Course:
Cross Training:			
How I Felt:			

Week 15 Wrap Up

WEEKLY SUMMARY		
Week Total:	Longest Run:	Shortest Run:
Average:	Monthly Total:	Yearly Total:
Daily Weight		

Mon	Tues	Wed	Thurs	Fri	sat	Sun

Morning Pulse

Mon	Tues	Wed	Thurs	Fri	sat	Sun

Did I meet my goals for the week?   ☐ Yes   ☐ No

What helped me reach my goals or what kept me from reaching my goals:

_____

_____

How do I feel about that? _____

_____

What will I change next week? _____

What will I not change next week? _____

Notes/Other Observations: _____

_____

_____

_____

_____

> *"Pick one thing each year that you need to improve, and work on that. It might be improving your diet, getting more sleep, or increasing your mileage. You can't work on everything at once."*
> **Bob Kennedy**

Week of ___/___/_____ - ___/___/_____

Goals for Week: _____

_____

_____

	Time	Distance	Pace	Weekly Total
MONDAY				
Time of Day	Weather	Route/Course:		
Cross Training:				
How I Felt:				

	Time	Distance	Pace	Weekly Total
TUESDAY				
Time of Day	Weather	Route/Course:		
Cross Training:				
How I Felt:				

	Time	Distance	Pace	Weekly Total
WEDNESDAY				
Time of Day	Weather	Route/Course:		
Cross Training:				
How I Felt:				

THURSDAY	Time	Distance	Pace	Weekly Total
Time of Day	Weather	Route/Course:		
Cross Training:				
How I Felt:				

FRIDAY	Time	Distance	Pace	Weekly Total
Time of Day	Weather	Route/Course:		
Cross Training:				
How I Felt:				

SATURDAY	Time	Distance	Pace	Weekly Total
Time of Day	Weather	Route/Course:		
Cross Training:				
How I Felt:				

SUNDAY	Time	Distance	Pace	Weekly Total
Time of Day	Weather	Route/Course:		
Cross Training:				
How I Felt:				

Week 16 Wrap Up

WEEKLY SUMMARY		
Week Total:	Longest Run:	Shortest Run:
Average:	Monthly Total:	Yearly Total:

Daily Weight						
Mon	Tues	Wed	Thurs	Fri	sat	Sun

Morning Pulse						
Mon	Tues	Wed	Thurs	Fri	sat	Sun

Did I meet my goals for the week?   ☐ Yes   ☐ No

What helped me reach my goals or what kept me from reaching my goals:

_____

_____

How do I feel about that? _____

_____

What will I change next week? _____

What will I not change next week? _____

Notes/Other Observations: _____

_____

_____

_____

_____

_____

"Relish the bad training runs. Without them it's difficult to recognize, much less appreciate, the good ones."

Pat Teske

Week of ___/___/_____ - ___/___/_____

Goals for Week: _____

_____

_____

MONDAY	Time	Distance	Pace	Weekly Total
Time of Day	Weather	Route/Course:		
Cross Training:				
How I Felt:				

TUESDAY	Time	Distance	Pace	Weekly Total
Time of Day	Weather	Route/Course:		
Cross Training:				
How I Felt:				

WEDNESDAY	Time	Distance	Pace	Weekly Total
Time of Day	Weather	Route/Course:		
Cross Training:				
How I Felt:				

THURSDAY	Time	Distance	Pace	Weekly Total
Time of Day	Weather	Route/Course:		
Cross Training:				
How I Felt:				

FRIDAY	Time	Distance	Pace	Weekly Total
Time of Day	Weather	Route/Course:		
Cross Training:				
How I Felt:				

SATURDAY	Time	Distance	Pace	Weekly Total
Time of Day	Weather	Route/Course:		
Cross Training:				
How I Felt:				

SUNDAY	Time	Distance	Pace	Weekly Total
Time of Day	Weather	Route/Course:		
Cross Training:				
How I Felt:				

Week 17 Wrap Up

WEEKLY SUMMARY		
Week Total:	Longest Run:	Shortest Run:
Average:	Monthly Total:	Yearly Total:
Daily Weight							
Mon	Tues	Wed	Thurs	Fri	sat	Sun
Morning Pulse							
Mon	Tues	Wed	Thurs	Fri	sat	Sun

Did I meet my goals for the week?   ☐ Yes   ☐ No

What helped me reach my goals or what kept me from reaching my goals:

_____

_____

How do I feel about that? _____

_____

What will I change next week? _____

What will I not change next week? _____

Notes/Other Observations: _____

_____

_____

_____

_____

> *"The idea that you can't lose contact with the leaders has cut more throats than it has saved."*
>
> **Arthur Lydiard**

Week of ___/___/_____ - ___/___/_____

Goals for Week: _____

_____

_____

MONDAY	Time	Distance	Pace	Weekly Total
Time of Day	Weather	Route/Course:		
Cross Training:				
How I Felt:				

TUESDAY	Time	Distance	Pace	Weekly Total
Time of Day	Weather	Route/Course:		
Cross Training:				
How I Felt:				

WEDNESDAY	Time	Distance	Pace	Weekly Total
Time of Day	Weather	Route/Course:		
Cross Training:				
How I Felt:				

THURSDAY	Time	Distance	Pace	Weekly Total

Time of Day	Weather	Route/Course:

Cross Training:

How I Felt:

FRIDAY	Time	Distance	Pace	Weekly Total

Time of Day	Weather	Route/Course:

Cross Training:

How I Felt:

SATURDAY	Time	Distance	Pace	Weekly Total

Time of Day	Weather	Route/Course:

Cross Training:

How I Felt:

SUNDAY	Time	Distance	Pace	Weekly Total

Time of Day	Weather	Route/Course:

Cross Training:

How I Felt:

Week 18 Wrap Up

WEEKLY SUMMARY							
Week Total:		Longest Run:			Shortest Run:		
Average:		Monthly Total:			Yearly Total:		
Daily Weight							
Mon	Tues	Wed	Thurs	Fri	sat	Sun	
Morning Pulse							
Mon	Tues	Wed	Thurs	Fri	sat	Sun	

Did I meet my goals for the week?   ☐ Yes   ☐ No

What helped me reach my goals or what kept me from reaching my goals:

_____

_____

How do I feel about that? _____

_____

What will I change next week? _____

What will I not change next week? _____

Notes/Other Observations: _____

_____

_____

_____

_____

_____

"Train like the athlete you want to be, not the athlete you are or used to be."

Pat Menzies

Week of ___/___/_____ - ___/___/_____

Goals for Week: _____

_____

_____

MONDAY	Time	Distance	Pace	Weekly Total
Time of Day	Weather	Route/Course:		
Cross Training:				
How I Felt:				

TUESDAY	Time	Distance	Pace	Weekly Total
Time of Day	Weather	Route/Course:		
Cross Training:				
How I Felt:				

WEDNESDAY	Time	Distance	Pace	Weekly Total
Time of Day	Weather	Route/Course:		
Cross Training:				
How I Felt:				

THURSDAY	Time	Distance	Pace	Weekly Total

Time of Day	Weather	Route/Course:

Cross Training:

How I Felt:

FRIDAY	Time	Distance	Pace	Weekly Total

Time of Day	Weather	Route/Course:

Cross Training:

How I Felt:

SATURDAY	Time	Distance	Pace	Weekly Total

Time of Day	Weather	Route/Course:

Cross Training:

How I Felt:

SUNDAY	Time	Distance	Pace	Weekly Total

Time of Day	Weather	Route/Course:

Cross Training:

How I Felt:

Week 19 Wrap Up

WEEKLY SUMMARY							
Week Total:		Longest Run:			Shortest Run:		
Average:		Monthly Total:			Yearly Total:		
Daily Weight							
Mon	Tues	Wed	Thurs	Fri	sat	Sun	
Morning Pulse							
Mon	Tues	Wed	Thurs	Fri	sat	Sun	

Did I meet my goals for the week? ☐ Yes ☐ No

What helped me reach my goals or what kept me from reaching my goals:

_____

_____

How do I feel about that? _____

_____

What will I change next week? _____

What will I not change next week? _____

Notes/Other Observations: _____

_____

_____

_____

_____

> *"It's better to run too slow at the start than too fast and get into oxygen debt, which is what 99.9 percent of runners do. You have to learn pace."*
>
> **Bill Bowerman**

Week of ___/___/_____ - ___/___/_____

Goals for Week: _____

_____

_____

MONDAY	Time	Distance	Pace	Weekly Total
Time of Day	Weather	Route/Course:		
Cross Training:				
How I Felt:				

TUESDAY	Time	Distance	Pace	Weekly Total
Time of Day	Weather	Route/Course:		
Cross Training:				
How I Felt:				

WEDNESDAY	Time	Distance	Pace	Weekly Total
Time of Day	Weather	Route/Course:		
Cross Training:				
How I Felt:				

THURSDAY	Time	Distance	Pace	Weekly Total

Time of Day	Weather	Route/Course:

Cross Training:

How I Felt:

FRIDAY	Time	Distance	Pace	Weekly Total

Time of Day	Weather	Route/Course:

Cross Training:

How I Felt:

SATURDAY	Time	Distance	Pace	Weekly Total

Time of Day	Weather	Route/Course:

Cross Training:

How I Felt:

SUNDAY	Time	Distance	Pace	Weekly Total

Time of Day	Weather	Route/Course:

Cross Training:

How I Felt:

Week 20 Wrap Up

WEEKLY SUMMARY								
Week Total:		Longest Run:				Shortest Run:		
Average:		Monthly Total:				Yearly Total:		
Daily Weight								
Mon	Tues	Wed	Thurs		Fri	sat		Sun
Morning Pulse								
Mon	Tues	Wed	Thurs		Fri	sat		Sun

Did I meet my goals for the week?   ☐ Yes   ☐ No

What helped me reach my goals or what kept me from reaching my goals:

_____

_____

How do I feel about that? _____

_____

What will I change next week? _____

What will I not change next week? _____

Notes/Other Observations: _____

_____

_____

_____

_____

_____

"Build up your mileage in gradual increments, but every third or fourth week, drop back in mileage to recover. This will help you avoid your breaking point."

Lee Fidler

Week of ___/___/_____ - ___/___/_____

Goals for Week: _____

_____

_____

MONDAY	Time	Distance	Pace	Weekly Total
Time of Day	Weather	Route/Course:		
Cross Training:				
How I Felt:				

TUESDAY	Time	Distance	Pace	Weekly Total
Time of Day	Weather	Route/Course:		
Cross Training:				
How I Felt:				

WEDNESDAY	Time	Distance	Pace	Weekly Total
Time of Day	Weather	Route/Course:		
Cross Training:				
How I Felt:				

THURSDAY	Time	Distance	Pace	Weekly Total

Time of Day	Weather	Route/Course:

Cross Training:

How I Felt:

FRIDAY	Time	Distance	Pace	Weekly Total

Time of Day	Weather	Route/Course:

Cross Training:

How I Felt:

SATURDAY	Time	Distance	Pace	Weekly Total

Time of Day	Weather	Route/Course:

Cross Training:

How I Felt:

SUNDAY	Time	Distance	Pace	Weekly Total

Time of Day	Weather	Route/Course:

Cross Training:

How I Felt:

Week 21 Wrap Up

WEEKLY SUMMARY							
Week Total:		Longest Run:			Shortest Run:		
Average:		Monthly Total:			Yearly Total:		
Daily Weight							
Mon	Tues	Wed	Thurs		Fri	sat	Sun
Morning Pulse							
Mon	Tues	Wed	Thurs		Fri	sat	Sun

Did I meet my goals for the week?   ☐ Yes   ☐ No

What helped me reach my goals or what kept me from reaching my goals:

_____

_____

How do I feel about that? _____

_____

What will I change next week? _____

What will I not change next week? _____

Notes/Other Observations: _____

_____

_____

_____

_____

_____

> *"You have a choice. You can throw in the towel, or you can use it to wipe the sweat off of your face."*
>
> **Gatorade commercial**

Week of ___/___/_____ - ___/___/_____

Goals for Week: _____

_____

_____

MONDAY	Time	Distance	Pace	Weekly Total
Time of Day	Weather	Route/Course:		
Cross Training:				
How I Felt:				

TUESDAY	Time	Distance	Pace	Weekly Total
Time of Day	Weather	Route/Course:		
Cross Training:				
How I Felt:				

WEDNESDAY	Time	Distance	Pace	Weekly Total
Time of Day	Weather	Route/Course:		
Cross Training:				
How I Felt:				

THURSDAY	Time	Distance	Pace	Weekly Total

Time of Day	Weather	Route/Course:

Cross Training:
How I Felt:

FRIDAY	Time	Distance	Pace	Weekly Total

Time of Day	Weather	Route/Course:

Cross Training:
How I Felt:

SATURDAY	Time	Distance	Pace	Weekly Total

Time of Day	Weather	Route/Course:

Cross Training:
How I Felt:

SUNDAY	Time	Distance	Pace	Weekly Total

Time of Day	Weather	Route/Course:

Cross Training:
How I Felt:

Week 22 Wrap Up

WEEKLY SUMMARY							
Week Total:		Longest Run:			Shortest Run:		
Average:		Monthly Total:			Yearly Total:		
Daily Weight							
Mon	Tues	Wed	Thurs	Fri	sat	Sun	
Morning Pulse							
Mon	Tues	Wed	Thurs	Fri	sat	Sun	

Did I meet my goals for the week?   ☐ Yes   ☐ No

What helped me reach my goals or what kept me from reaching my goals:

_____

_____

How do I feel about that? _____

_____

What will I change next week? _____

What will I not change next week? _____

Notes/Other Observations: _____

_____

_____

_____

_____

_____

"Running is a 'no B.S.' sport. You earn the success you achieve. There's no way to fake it. You must do the work, put in the time. There is no other way."

Kevin Nelson

Week of ___/___/_____ - ___/___/_____

Goals for Week: _____

_____

_____

	Time	Distance	Pace	Weekly Total
MONDAY				
Time of Day	Weather	Route/Course:		
Cross Training:				
How I Felt:				

	Time	Distance	Pace	Weekly Total
TUESDAY				
Time of Day	Weather	Route/Course:		
Cross Training:				
How I Felt:				

	Time	Distance	Pace	Weekly Total
WEDNESDAY				
Time of Day	Weather	Route/Course:		
Cross Training:				
How I Felt:				

THURSDAY	Time	Distance	Pace	Weekly Total

Time of Day	Weather	Route/Course:		

Cross Training:

How I Felt:

FRIDAY	Time	Distance	Pace	Weekly Total

Time of Day	Weather	Route/Course:		

Cross Training:

How I Felt:

SATURDAY	Time	Distance	Pace	Weekly Total

Time of Day	Weather	Route/Course:		

Cross Training:

How I Felt:

SUNDAY	Time	Distance	Pace	Weekly Total

Time of Day	Weather	Route/Course:		

Cross Training:

How I Felt:

Week 23 Wrap Up

WEEKLY SUMMARY		
Week Total:	Longest Run:	Shortest Run:
Average:	Monthly Total:	Yearly Total:
Daily Weight						
Mon	Tues	Wed	Thurs	Fri	sat	Sun
Morning Pulse						
Mon	Tues	Wed	Thurs	Fri	sat	Sun

Did I meet my goals for the week? ☐ Yes   ☐ No

What helped me reach my goals or what kept me from reaching my goals:

_____

_____

How do I feel about that? _____

_____

What will I change next week? _____

What will I not change next week? _____

Notes/Other Observations: _____

_____

_____

_____

_____

_____

> *"Visualizing perfect running form will help you stay relaxed. Visualize before the race. Then, once you're in the race, pick out someone who's looking good and running relaxed. This will help you do the same."*
>
> **Gayle Barron**

Week of ___/___/_____ - ___/___/_____

Goals for Week: _____

_____

_____

	Time	Distance	Pace	Weekly Total
MONDAY				
Time of Day	Weather	Route/Course:		
Cross Training:				
How I Felt:				

	Time	Distance	Pace	Weekly Total
TUESDAY				
Time of Day	Weather	Route/Course:		
Cross Training:				
How I Felt:				

	Time	Distance	Pace	Weekly Total
WEDNESDAY				
Time of Day	Weather	Route/Course:		
Cross Training:				
How I Felt:				

THURSDAY	Time	Distance	Pace	Weekly Total

Time of Day	Weather	Route/Course:

Cross Training:
How I Felt:

FRIDAY	Time	Distance	Pace	Weekly Total

Time of Day	Weather	Route/Course:

Cross Training:
How I Felt:

SATURDAY	Time	Distance	Pace	Weekly Total

Time of Day	Weather	Route/Course:

Cross Training:
How I Felt:

SUNDAY	Time	Distance	Pace	Weekly Total

Time of Day	Weather	Route/Course:

Cross Training:
How I Felt:

Week 24 Wrap Up

WEEKLY SUMMARY						
Week Total:		Longest Run:			Shortest Run:	
Average:		Monthly Total:			Yearly Total:	
Daily Weight						
Mon	Tues	Wed	Thurs	Fri	sat	Sun
Morning Pulse						
Mon	Tues	Wed	Thurs	Fri	sat	Sun

Did I meet my goals for the week? ☐ Yes   ☐ No

What helped me reach my goals or what kept me from reaching my goals:

_____

_____

How do I feel about that? _____

_____

What will I change next week? _____

What will I not change next week? _____

Notes/Other Observations: _____

_____

_____

_____

_____

*"Quality counts, if you want to stay fast.
Don't do all your workouts in the comfort zone."*

Ken Sparks, Ph.D

Week of ___/___/_____ - ___/___/_____

Goals for Week: _____

_____

_____

MONDAY	Time	Distance	Pace	Weekly Total
Time of Day	Weather	Route/Course:		
Cross Training:				
How I Felt:				

TUESDAY	Time	Distance	Pace	Weekly Total
Time of Day	Weather	Route/Course:		
Cross Training:				
How I Felt:				

WEDNESDAY	Time	Distance	Pace	Weekly Total
Time of Day	Weather	Route/Course:		
Cross Training:				
How I Felt:				

THURSDAY	Time	Distance	Pace	Weekly Total

Time of Day	Weather	Route/Course:		

Cross Training:

How I Felt:

FRIDAY	Time	Distance	Pace	Weekly Total

Time of Day	Weather	Route/Course:		

Cross Training:

How I Felt:

SATURDAY	Time	Distance	Pace	Weekly Total

Time of Day	Weather	Route/Course:		

Cross Training:

How I Felt:

SUNDAY	Time	Distance	Pace	Weekly Total

Time of Day	Weather	Route/Course:		

Cross Training:

How I Felt:

Week 25 Wrap Up

WEEKLY SUMMARY							
Week Total:		Longest Run:			Shortest Run:		
Average:		Monthly Total:			Yearly Total:		
Daily Weight							
Mon	Tues	Wed	Thurs		Fri	sat	Sun
Morning Pulse							
Mon	Tues	Wed	Thurs		Fri	sat	Sun

Did I meet my goals for the week? ☐ Yes   ☐ No

What helped me reach my goals or what kept me from reaching my goals:

_____

_____

How do I feel about that? _____

_____

What will I change next week? _____

What will I not change next week? _____

Notes/Other Observations: _____

_____

_____

_____

_____

> *"Running is my private time, my therapy, my religion."*
> **Gail W. Kislevitz**

Week of ___/___/_____ - ___/___/_____

Goals for Week: _____

_____

_____

MONDAY	Time	Distance	Pace	Weekly Total
Time of Day	Weather	Route/Course:		
Cross Training:				
How I Felt:				

TUESDAY	Time	Distance	Pace	Weekly Total
Time of Day	Weather	Route/Course:		
Cross Training:				
How I Felt:				

WEDNESDAY	Time	Distance	Pace	Weekly Total
Time of Day	Weather	Route/Course:		
Cross Training:				
How I Felt:				

THURSDAY	Time	Distance	Pace	Weekly Total

Time of Day	Weather	Route/Course:

Cross Training:

How I Felt:

FRIDAY	Time	Distance	Pace	Weekly Total

Time of Day	Weather	Route/Course:

Cross Training:

How I Felt:

SATURDAY	Time	Distance	Pace	Weekly Total

Time of Day	Weather	Route/Course:

Cross Training:

How I Felt:

SUNDAY	Time	Distance	Pace	Weekly Total

Time of Day	Weather	Route/Course:

Cross Training:

How I Felt:

Week 26 Wrap Up

WEEKLY SUMMARY				
Week Total:	Longest Run:		Shortest Run:	
Average:	Monthly Total:		Yearly Total:	
Daily Weight				
Mon	Tues	Wed	Thurs	Fri	sat	Sun
Morning Pulse				
Mon	Tues	Wed	Thurs	Fri	sat	Sun

Did I meet my goals for the week?   ☐ Yes   ☐ No

What helped me reach my goals or what kept me from reaching my goals:

_____

_____

How do I feel about that? _____

_____

What will I change next week? _____

What will I not change next week? _____

Notes/Other Observations: _____

_____

_____

_____

_____

_____

> *"Running is a big question mark that's there each and every day. It asks you, 'Are you going to be a wimp or are you going to be strong today?'"*
>
> **Peter Maher**

Week of ___/___/_____ - ___/___/_____

Goals for Week: _____

_____

_____

MONDAY	Time	Distance	Pace	Weekly Total
Time of Day	Weather	Route/Course:		
Cross Training:				
How I Felt:				

TUESDAY	Time	Distance	Pace	Weekly Total
Time of Day	Weather	Route/Course:		
Cross Training:				
How I Felt:				

WEDNESDAY	Time	Distance	Pace	Weekly Total
Time of Day	Weather	Route/Course:		
Cross Training:				
How I Felt:				

THURSDAY	Time	Distance	Pace	Weekly Total

Time of Day	Weather	Route/Course:

Cross Training:

How I Felt:

FRIDAY	Time	Distance	Pace	Weekly Total

Time of Day	Weather	Route/Course:

Cross Training:

How I Felt:

SATURDAY	Time	Distance	Pace	Weekly Total

Time of Day	Weather	Route/Course:

Cross Training:

How I Felt:

SUNDAY	Time	Distance	Pace	Weekly Total

Time of Day	Weather	Route/Course:

Cross Training:

How I Felt:

Week 27 Wrap Up

WEEKLY SUMMARY						
Week Total:			Longest Run:			Shortest Run:
Average:			Monthly Total:			Yearly Total:
Daily Weight						
Mon	Tues	Wed	Thurs	Fri	sat	Sun
Morning Pulse						
Mon	Tues	Wed	Thurs	Fri	sat	Sun

Did I meet my goals for the week?   ☐ Yes   ☐ No

What helped me reach my goals or what kept me from reaching my goals:

_____

_____

How do I feel about that? _____

_____

What will I change next week? _____

What will I not change next week? _____

Notes/Other Observations: _____

_____

_____

_____

_____

_____

> *"Slip in behind someone running a similar pace and, yes, draft. It's not illegal. It's not even poor form. On the contrary, it's just plain smart."*
>
> **Priscilla Welch**

Week of ___/___/_____ - ___/___/_____

Goals for Week: _____

_____

_____

MONDAY	Time	Distance	Pace	Weekly Total
Time of Day	Weather	Route/Course:		
Cross Training:				
How I Felt:				

TUESDAY	Time	Distance	Pace	Weekly Total
Time of Day	Weather	Route/Course:		
Cross Training:				
How I Felt:				

WEDNESDAY	Time	Distance	Pace	Weekly Total
Time of Day	Weather	Route/Course:		
Cross Training:				
How I Felt:				

THURSDAY	Time	Distance	Pace	Weekly Total
Time of Day	Weather	Route/Course:		
Cross Training:				
How I Felt:				

FRIDAY	Time	Distance	Pace	Weekly Total
Time of Day	Weather	Route/Course:		
Cross Training:				
How I Felt:				

SATURDAY	Time	Distance	Pace	Weekly Total
Time of Day	Weather	Route/Course:		
Cross Training:				
How I Felt:				

SUNDAY	Time	Distance	Pace	Weekly Total
Time of Day	Weather	Route/Course:		
Cross Training:				
How I Felt:				

Week 28 Wrap Up

WEEKLY SUMMARY						
Week Total:		Longest Run:			Shortest Run:	
Average:		Monthly Total:			Yearly Total:	
Daily Weight						
Mon	Tues	Wed	Thurs	Fri	sat	Sun
Morning Pulse						
Mon	Tues	Wed	Thurs	Fri	sat	Sun

Did I meet my goals for the week?   ☐ Yes   ☐ No

What helped me reach my goals or what kept me from reaching my goals:

_____

_____

How do I feel about that? _____

_____

What will I change next week? _____

What will I not change next week? _____

Notes/Other Observations: _____

_____

_____

_____

_____

_____

> *"It's very hard in the beginning to understand that the whole idea is not to beat the other runners. Eventually you learn that the competition is against the little voice inside you that wants you to quit."*
>
> **George Sheehan**

Week of ___/___/_____ - ___/___/_____

Goals for Week: _____

_____

_____

MONDAY	Time	Distance	Pace	Weekly Total
Time of Day	Weather	Route/Course:		
Cross Training:				
How I Felt:				

TUESDAY	Time	Distance	Pace	Weekly Total
Time of Day	Weather	Route/Course:		
Cross Training:				
How I Felt:				

WEDNESDAY	Time	Distance	Pace	Weekly Total
Time of Day	Weather	Route/Course:		
Cross Training:				
How I Felt:				

THURSDAY	Time	Distance	Pace	Weekly Total
Time of Day	Weather	Route/Course:		
Cross Training:				
How I Felt:				

FRIDAY	Time	Distance	Pace	Weekly Total
Time of Day	Weather	Route/Course:		
Cross Training:				
How I Felt:				

SATURDAY	Time	Distance	Pace	Weekly Total
Time of Day	Weather	Route/Course:		
Cross Training:				
How I Felt:				

SUNDAY	Time	Distance	Pace	Weekly Total
Time of Day	Weather	Route/Course:		
Cross Training:				
How I Felt:				

Week 29 Wrap Up

WEEKLY SUMMARY							
Week Total:		Longest Run:			Shortest Run:		
Average:		Monthly Total:			Yearly Total:		
Daily Weight							
Mon	Tues	Wed	Thurs	Fri	sat	Sun	
Morning Pulse							
Mon	Tues	Wed	Thurs	Fri	sat	Sun	

Did I meet my goals for the week?   ☐ Yes   ☐ No

What helped me reach my goals or what kept me from reaching my goals:

_____

_____

How do I feel about that? _____

_____

What will I change next week? _____

What will I not change next week? _____

Notes/Other Observations: _____

_____

_____

_____

_____

"The will to win means nothing without the will to prepare."

Juma Ikangaa

Week of ___/___/_____ - ___/___/_____

Goals for Week: _____

_____

_____

	Time	Distance	Pace	Weekly Total
MONDAY				
Time of Day	Weather	Route/Course:		
Cross Training:				
How I Felt:				

	Time	Distance	Pace	Weekly Total
TUESDAY				
Time of Day	Weather	Route/Course:		
Cross Training:				
How I Felt:				

	Time	Distance	Pace	Weekly Total
WEDNESDAY				
Time of Day	Weather	Route/Course:		
Cross Training:				
How I Felt:				

THURSDAY	Time	Distance	Pace	Weekly Total

Time of Day	Weather	Route/Course:

Cross Training:

How I Felt:

FRIDAY	Time	Distance	Pace	Weekly Total

Time of Day	Weather	Route/Course:

Cross Training:

How I Felt:

SATURDAY	Time	Distance	Pace	Weekly Total

Time of Day	Weather	Route/Course:

Cross Training:

How I Felt:

SUNDAY	Time	Distance	Pace	Weekly Total

Time of Day	Weather	Route/Course:

Cross Training:

How I Felt:

Week 30 Wrap Up

WEEKLY SUMMARY							
Week Total:		Longest Run:			Shortest Run:		
Average:		Monthly Total:			Yearly Total:		
Daily Weight							
Mon	Tues	Wed	Thurs	Fri	sat		Sun
Morning Pulse							
Mon	Tues	Wed	Thurs	Fri	sat		Sun

Did I meet my goals for the week? ☐ Yes   ☐ No

What helped me reach my goals or what kept me from reaching my goals:

_____

_____

How do I feel about that? _____

_____

What will I change next week? _____

What will I not change next week? _____

Notes/Other Observations: _____

_____

_____

_____

_____

"Pain is inevitable. Suffering is optional".

Haruki Murakami

Week of ___/___/_____ - ___/___/_____

Goals for Week: _____

_____

_____

MONDAY	Time	Distance	Pace	Weekly Total

Time of Day	Weather	Route/Course:

Cross Training:
How I Felt:

TUESDAY	Time	Distance	Pace	Weekly Total

Time of Day	Weather	Route/Course:

Cross Training:
How I Felt:

WEDNESDAY	Time	Distance	Pace	Weekly Total

Time of Day	Weather	Route/Course:

Cross Training:
How I Felt:

THURSDAY	Time	Distance	Pace	Weekly Total

Time of Day	Weather	Route/Course:

Cross Training:

How I Felt:

FRIDAY	Time	Distance	Pace	Weekly Total

Time of Day	Weather	Route/Course:

Cross Training:

How I Felt:

SATURDAY	Time	Distance	Pace	Weekly Total

Time of Day	Weather	Route/Course:

Cross Training:

How I Felt:

SUNDAY	Time	Distance	Pace	Weekly Total

Time of Day	Weather	Route/Course:

Cross Training:

How I Felt:

Week 31 Wrap Up

WEEKLY SUMMARY						
Week Total:		Longest Run:			Shortest Run:	
Average:		Monthly Total:			Yearly Total:	
Daily Weight						
Mon	Tues	Wed	Thurs	Fri	sat	Sun
Morning Pulse						
Mon	Tues	Wed	Thurs	Fri	sat	Sun

Did I meet my goals for the week?   ☐ Yes   ☐ No

What helped me reach my goals or what kept me from reaching my goals:

_____

_____

How do I feel about that? _____

_____

What will I change next week? _____

What will I not change next week? _____

Notes/Other Observations: _____

_____

_____

_____

_____

_____

> *"The best pace is a suicide pace,
> and today looks like a good day to die."*
>
> **Steve Prefontaine**

Week of ___/___/_____ - ___/___/_____

Goals for Week: _____

_____

_____

MONDAY	Time	Distance	Pace	Weekly Total
Time of Day	Weather	Route/Course:		
Cross Training:				
How I Felt:				

TUESDAY	Time	Distance	Pace	Weekly Total
Time of Day	Weather	Route/Course:		
Cross Training:				
How I Felt:				

WEDNESDAY	Time	Distance	Pace	Weekly Total
Time of Day	Weather	Route/Course:		
Cross Training:				
How I Felt:				

THURSDAY	Time	Distance	Pace	Weekly Total
Time of Day	Weather	Route/Course:		
Cross Training:				
How I Felt:				

FRIDAY	Time	Distance	Pace	Weekly Total
Time of Day	Weather	Route/Course:		
Cross Training:				
How I Felt:				

SATURDAY	Time	Distance	Pace	Weekly Total
Time of Day	Weather	Route/Course:		
Cross Training:				
How I Felt:				

SUNDAY	Time	Distance	Pace	Weekly Total
Time of Day	Weather	Route/Course:		
Cross Training:				
How I Felt:				

Week 32 Wrap Up

WEEKLY SUMMARY							
Week Total:		Longest Run:			Shortest Run:		
Average:		Monthly Total:			Yearly Total:		
Daily Weight							
Mon	Tues	Wed	Thurs		Fri	sat	Sun
Morning Pulse							
Mon	Tues	Wed	Thurs		Fri	sat	Sun

Did I meet my goals for the week?   ☐ Yes   ☐ No

What helped me reach my goals or what kept me from reaching my goals:

_____

_____

How do I feel about that? _____

_____

What will I change next week? _____

What will I not change next week? _____

Notes/Other Observations: _____

_____

_____

_____

_____

_____

> *"The miracle isn't that I finished. The miracle is that I had the courage to start."*
>
> **John Bingham**

Week of ___/___/_____ - ___/___/_____

Goals for Week: _____

_____

_____

MONDAY	Time	Distance	Pace	Weekly Total
Time of Day	Weather	Route/Course:		
Cross Training:				
How I Felt:				

TUESDAY	Time	Distance	Pace	Weekly Total
Time of Day	Weather	Route/Course:		
Cross Training:				
How I Felt:				

WEDNESDAY	Time	Distance	Pace	Weekly Total
Time of Day	Weather	Route/Course:		
Cross Training:				
How I Felt:				

THURSDAY	Time	Distance	Pace	Weekly Total
Time of Day	Weather	Route/Course:		
Cross Training:				
How I Felt:				

FRIDAY	Time	Distance	Pace	Weekly Total
Time of Day	Weather	Route/Course:		
Cross Training:				
How I Felt:				

SATURDAY	Time	Distance	Pace	Weekly Total
Time of Day	Weather	Route/Course:		
Cross Training:				
How I Felt:				

SUNDAY	Time	Distance	Pace	Weekly Total
Time of Day	Weather	Route/Course:		
Cross Training:				
How I Felt:				

Week 33 Wrap Up

WEEKLY SUMMARY							
Week Total:		Longest Run:			Shortest Run:		
Average:		Monthly Total:			Yearly Total:		
Daily Weight							
Mon	Tues	Wed	Thurs	Fri	sat	Sun	
Morning Pulse							
Mon	Tues	Wed	Thurs	Fri	sat	Sun	

Did I meet my goals for the week?   ☐ Yes   ☐ No

What helped me reach my goals or what kept me from reaching my goals:

_____

_____

How do I feel about that? _____

_____

What will I change next week? _____

What will I not change next week? _____

Notes/Other Observations: _____

_____

_____

_____

_____

_____

> *"Ask yourself: 'Can I give more?'.*
> *The answer is usually: 'Yes'."*
>
> **Paul Tergat**

Week of ___/___/_____ - ___/___/_____

Goals for Week: _____

_____

_____

	Time	Distance	Pace	Weekly Total
MONDAY				
Time of Day	Weather	Route/Course:		
Cross Training:				
How I Felt:				

	Time	Distance	Pace	Weekly Total
TUESDAY				
Time of Day	Weather	Route/Course:		
Cross Training:				
How I Felt:				

	Time	Distance	Pace	Weekly Total
WEDNESDAY				
Time of Day	Weather	Route/Course:		
Cross Training:				
How I Felt:				

THURSDAY	Time	Distance	Pace	Weekly Total

Time of Day	Weather	Route/Course:

Cross Training:

How I Felt:

FRIDAY	Time	Distance	Pace	Weekly Total

Time of Day	Weather	Route/Course:

Cross Training:

How I Felt:

SATURDAY	Time	Distance	Pace	Weekly Total

Time of Day	Weather	Route/Course:

Cross Training:

How I Felt:

SUNDAY	Time	Distance	Pace	Weekly Total

Time of Day	Weather	Route/Course:

Cross Training:

How I Felt:

Week 34 Wrap Up

WEEKLY SUMMARY							
Week Total:		Longest Run:			Shortest Run:		
Average:		Monthly Total:			Yearly Total:		
Daily Weight							
Mon	Tues	Wed	Thurs	Fri	sat	Sun	
Morning Pulse							
Mon	Tues	Wed	Thurs	Fri	sat	Sun	

Did I meet my goals for the week?   ☐ Yes   ☐ No

What helped me reach my goals or what kept me from reaching my goals:

_____

_____

How do I feel about that? _____

_____

What will I change next week? _____

What will I not change next week? _____

Notes/Other Observations: _____

_____

_____

_____

_____

_____

> *"A run begins the moment you forget you are running."*
>
> **Adidas**

Week of ___/___/_____ - ___/___/_____

Goals for Week: _____

_____

_____

MONDAY	Time	Distance	Pace	Weekly Total

Time of Day	Weather	Route/Course:

Cross Training:
How I Felt:

TUESDAY	Time	Distance	Pace	Weekly Total

Time of Day	Weather	Route/Course:

Cross Training:
How I Felt:

WEDNESDAY	Time	Distance	Pace	Weekly Total

Time of Day	Weather	Route/Course:

Cross Training:
How I Felt:

THURSDAY	Time	Distance	Pace	Weekly Total
Time of Day	Weather	Route/Course:		
Cross Training:				
How I Felt:				

FRIDAY	Time	Distance	Pace	Weekly Total
Time of Day	Weather	Route/Course:		
Cross Training:				
How I Felt:				

SATURDAY	Time	Distance	Pace	Weekly Total
Time of Day	Weather	Route/Course:		
Cross Training:				
How I Felt:				

SUNDAY	Time	Distance	Pace	Weekly Total
Time of Day	Weather	Route/Course:		
Cross Training:				
How I Felt:				

Week 35 Wrap Up

WEEKLY SUMMARY						
Week Total:		Longest Run:			Shortest Run:	
Average:		Monthly Total:			Yearly Total:	
Daily Weight						
Mon	Tues	Wed	Thurs	Fri	sat	Sun
Morning Pulse						
Mon	Tues	Wed	Thurs	Fri	sat	Sun

Did I meet my goals for the week?   ☐ Yes   ☐ No

What helped me reach my goals or what kept me from reaching my goals:

_____

_____

How do I feel about that? _____

_____

What will I change next week? _____

What will I not change next week? _____

Notes/Other Observations: _____

_____

_____

_____

_____

> *"It's a treat being a runner, out in the world by yourself with not a soul to make you bad-tempered or tell you what to do."*
>
> **Alan Sillitoe**

Week of ___/___/_____ - ___/___/_____

Goals for Week: _____

_____

_____

MONDAY	Time	Distance	Pace	Weekly Total
Time of Day	Weather	Route/Course:		
Cross Training:				
How I Felt:				

TUESDAY	Time	Distance	Pace	Weekly Total
Time of Day	Weather	Route/Course:		
Cross Training:				
How I Felt:				

WEDNESDAY	Time	Distance	Pace	Weekly Total
Time of Day	Weather	Route/Course:		
Cross Training:				
How I Felt:				

THURSDAY	Time	Distance	Pace	Weekly Total
Time of Day	Weather	Route/Course:		
Cross Training:				
How I Felt:				

FRIDAY	Time	Distance	Pace	Weekly Total
Time of Day	Weather	Route/Course:		
Cross Training:				
How I Felt:				

SATURDAY	Time	Distance	Pace	Weekly Total
Time of Day	Weather	Route/Course:		
Cross Training:				
How I Felt:				

SUNDAY	Time	Distance	Pace	Weekly Total
Time of Day	Weather	Route/Course:		
Cross Training:				
How I Felt:				

Week 36 Wrap Up

WEEKLY SUMMARY		
Week Total:	Longest Run:	Shortest Run:
Average:	Monthly Total:	Yearly Total:

Daily Weight						
Mon	Tues	Wed	Thurs	Fri	sat	Sun

Morning Pulse						
Mon	Tues	Wed	Thurs	Fri	sat	Sun

Did I meet my goals for the week? ☐ Yes ☐ No

What helped me reach my goals or what kept me from reaching my goals:

_____

_____

How do I feel about that? _____

_____

What will I change next week? _____

What will I not change next week? _____

Notes/Other Observations: _____

_____

_____

_____

_____

_____

"Part of a runner's training consists of pushing back the limits of his mind."

Kenny Moore

Week of ___/___/_____ - ___/___/_____

Goals for Week: _____

_____

_____

MONDAY	Time	Distance	Pace	Weekly Total
Time of Day	Weather	Route/Course:		
Cross Training:				
How I Felt:				

TUESDAY	Time	Distance	Pace	Weekly Total
Time of Day	Weather	Route/Course:		
Cross Training:				
How I Felt:				

WEDNESDAY	Time	Distance	Pace	Weekly Total
Time of Day	Weather	Route/Course:		
Cross Training:				
How I Felt:				

THURSDAY	Time	Distance	Pace	Weekly Total
Time of Day	Weather	Route/Course:		
Cross Training:				
How I Felt:				

FRIDAY	Time	Distance	Pace	Weekly Total
Time of Day	Weather	Route/Course:		
Cross Training:				
How I Felt:				

SATURDAY	Time	Distance	Pace	Weekly Total
Time of Day	Weather	Route/Course:		
Cross Training:				
How I Felt:				

SUNDAY	Time	Distance	Pace	Weekly Total
Time of Day	Weather	Route/Course:		
Cross Training:				
How I Felt:				

Week 37 Wrap Up

WEEKLY SUMMARY						
Week Total:		Longest Run:			Shortest Run:	
Average:		Monthly Total:			Yearly Total:	
Daily Weight						
Mon	Tues	Wed	Thurs	Fri	sat	Sun
Morning Pulse						
Mon	Tues	Wed	Thurs	Fri	sat	Sun

Did I meet my goals for the week?   ☐ Yes   ☐ No

What helped me reach my goals or what kept me from reaching my goals:

_____

_____

How do I feel about that? _____

_____

What will I change next week? _____

What will I not change next week? _____

Notes/Other Observations: _____

_____

_____

_____

_____

_____

> *"It may seem odd to hear a coach say this, but I think a really great training partner is more important than a coach."*
>
> **Joan Nesbit**

Week of ___/___/_____ - ___/___/_____

Goals for Week: _____

_____

_____

MONDAY	Time	Distance	Pace	Weekly Total
Time of Day	Weather	Route/Course:		
Cross Training:				
How I Felt:				

TUESDAY	Time	Distance	Pace	Weekly Total
Time of Day	Weather	Route/Course:		
Cross Training:				
How I Felt:				

WEDNESDAY	Time	Distance	Pace	Weekly Total
Time of Day	Weather	Route/Course:		
Cross Training:				
How I Felt:				

THURSDAY	Time	Distance	Pace	Weekly Total

Time of Day	Weather	Route/Course:

Cross Training:

How I Felt:

FRIDAY	Time	Distance	Pace	Weekly Total

Time of Day	Weather	Route/Course:

Cross Training:

How I Felt:

SATURDAY	Time	Distance	Pace	Weekly Total

Time of Day	Weather	Route/Course:

Cross Training:

How I Felt:

SUNDAY	Time	Distance	Pace	Weekly Total

Time of Day	Weather	Route/Course:

Cross Training:

How I Felt:

Week 38 Wrap Up

WEEKLY SUMMARY		
Week Total:	Longest Run:	Shortest Run:
Average:	Monthly Total:	Yearly Total:

Daily Weight						
Mon	Tues	Wed	Thurs	Fri	sat	Sun

Morning Pulse						
Mon	Tues	Wed	Thurs	Fri	sat	Sun

Did I meet my goals for the week?   ☐ Yes   ☐ No

What helped me reach my goals or what kept me from reaching my goals:

_____

_____

How do I feel about that? _____

_____

What will I change next week? _____

What will I not change next week? _____

Notes/Other Observations: _____

_____

_____

_____

_____

_____

"If you can't win, make the fellow ahead of you break the record."

Unknown

Week of ___/___/_____ - ___/___/_____

Goals for Week: _____

_____

_____

MONDAY	Time	Distance	Pace	Weekly Total
Time of Day	Weather	Route/Course:		
Cross Training:				
How I Felt:				

TUESDAY	Time	Distance	Pace	Weekly Total
Time of Day	Weather	Route/Course:		
Cross Training:				
How I Felt:				

WEDNESDAY	Time	Distance	Pace	Weekly Total
Time of Day	Weather	Route/Course:		
Cross Training:				
How I Felt:				

THURSDAY	Time	Distance	Pace	Weekly Total
Time of Day	Weather	Route/Course:		
Cross Training:				
How I Felt:				

FRIDAY	Time	Distance	Pace	Weekly Total
Time of Day	Weather	Route/Course:		
Cross Training:				
How I Felt:				

SATURDAY	Time	Distance	Pace	Weekly Total
Time of Day	Weather	Route/Course:		
Cross Training:				
How I Felt:				

SUNDAY	Time	Distance	Pace	Weekly Total
Time of Day	Weather	Route/Course:		
Cross Training:				
How I Felt:				

Week 39 Wrap Up

WEEKLY SUMMARY							
Week Total:		Longest Run:			Shortest Run:		
Average:		Monthly Total:			Yearly Total:		
Daily Weight							
Mon	Tues	Wed	Thurs		Fri	sat	Sun
Morning Pulse							
Mon	Tues	Wed	Thurs		Fri	sat	Sun

Did I meet my goals for the week?   ☐ Yes   ☐ No

What helped me reach my goals or what kept me from reaching my goals:

_____

_____

How do I feel about that? _____

_____

What will I change next week? _____

What will I not change next week? _____

Notes/Other Observations: _____

_____

_____

_____

_____

_____

*"You don't run against a bloody stop watch, do you hear?
A runner runs against himself, against the best that's in him.
Not against a dead thing of wheels and pulleys.
That's the way to be great, running against yourself.
Against all the rotten mess in the world.
Against God, if you're good enough."*

Bill Persons

Week of ___/___/_____ - ___/___/_____

Goals for Week: _____

_____

_____

MONDAY	Time	Distance	Pace	Weekly Total
Time of Day	Weather	Route/Course:		
Cross Training:				
How I Felt:				

TUESDAY	Time	Distance	Pace	Weekly Total
Time of Day	Weather	Route/Course:		
Cross Training:				
How I Felt:				

WEDNESDAY	Time	Distance	Pace	Weekly Total
Time of Day	Weather	Route/Course:		
Cross Training:				
How I Felt:				

THURSDAY	Time	Distance	Pace	Weekly Total
Time of Day	Weather	Route/Course:		
Cross Training:				
How I Felt:				

FRIDAY	Time	Distance	Pace	Weekly Total
Time of Day	Weather	Route/Course:		
Cross Training:				
How I Felt:				

SATURDAY	Time	Distance	Pace	Weekly Total
Time of Day	Weather	Route/Course:		
Cross Training:				
How I Felt:				

SUNDAY	Time	Distance	Pace	Weekly Total
Time of Day	Weather	Route/Course:		
Cross Training:				
How I Felt:				

Week 40 Wrap Up

WEEKLY SUMMARY							
Week Total:		Longest Run:			Shortest Run:		
Average:		Monthly Total:			Yearly Total:		
Daily Weight							
Mon	Tues	Wed	Thurs		Fri	sat	Sun
Morning Pulse							
Mon	Tues	Wed	Thurs		Fri	sat	Sun

Did I meet my goals for the week? ☐ Yes ☐ No

What helped me reach my goals or what kept me from reaching my goals:

_____

_____

How do I feel about that? _____

_____

What will I change next week? _____

What will I not change next week? _____

Notes/Other Observations: _____

_____

_____

_____

_____

"Racing teaches us to challenge ourselves. It teaches us to push beyond where we thought we could go. It helps us to find out what we are made of. This is what we do. This is what it's all about."

PattiSue Plumer

Week of ___/___/_____ - ___/___/_____

Goals for Week: _____

_____

_____

MONDAY	Time	Distance	Pace	Weekly Total
Time of Day	Weather	Route/Course:		
Cross Training:				
How I Felt:				

TUESDAY	Time	Distance	Pace	Weekly Total
Time of Day	Weather	Route/Course:		
Cross Training:				
How I Felt:				

WEDNESDAY	Time	Distance	Pace	Weekly Total
Time of Day	Weather	Route/Course:		
Cross Training:				
How I Felt:				

THURSDAY	Time	Distance	Pace	Weekly Total

Time of Day	Weather	Route/Course:

Cross Training:

How I Felt:

FRIDAY	Time	Distance	Pace	Weekly Total

Time of Day	Weather	Route/Course:

Cross Training:

How I Felt:

SATURDAY	Time	Distance	Pace	Weekly Total

Time of Day	Weather	Route/Course:

Cross Training:

How I Felt:

SUNDAY	Time	Distance	Pace	Weekly Total

Time of Day	Weather	Route/Course:

Cross Training:

How I Felt:

Week 41 Wrap Up

WEEKLY SUMMARY							
Week Total:		Longest Run:			Shortest Run:		
Average:		Monthly Total:			Yearly Total:		
Daily Weight							
Mon	Tues	Wed	Thurs		Fri	sat	Sun
Morning Pulse							
Mon	Tues	Wed	Thurs		Fri	sat	Sun

Did I meet my goals for the week?   ☐ Yes   ☐ No

What helped me reach my goals or what kept me from reaching my goals:

_____

_____

How do I feel about that? _____

_____

What will I change next week? _____

What will I not change next week? _____

Notes/Other Observations: _____

_____

_____

_____

_____

_____

"Experience has taught me how important it is to just keep going, focusing on running fast and relaxed. Eventually pain passes and the flow returns. It's part of racing."

Frank Shorter

Week of ___/___/_____ - ___/___/_____

Goals for Week: _____

_____

_____

MONDAY	Time	Distance	Pace	Weekly Total
Time of Day	Weather	Route/Course:		
Cross Training:				
How I Felt:				

TUESDAY	Time	Distance	Pace	Weekly Total
Time of Day	Weather	Route/Course:		
Cross Training:				
How I Felt:				

WEDNESDAY	Time	Distance	Pace	Weekly Total
Time of Day	Weather	Route/Course:		
Cross Training:				
How I Felt:				

THURSDAY	Time	Distance	Pace	Weekly Total

Time of Day	Weather	Route/Course:

Cross Training:
How I Felt:

FRIDAY	Time	Distance	Pace	Weekly Total

Time of Day	Weather	Route/Course:

Cross Training:
How I Felt:

SATURDAY	Time	Distance	Pace	Weekly Total

Time of Day	Weather	Route/Course:

Cross Training:
How I Felt:

SUNDAY	Time	Distance	Pace	Weekly Total

Time of Day	Weather	Route/Course:

Cross Training:
How I Felt:

Week 42 Wrap Up

WEEKLY SUMMARY							
Week Total:		Longest Run:			Shortest Run:		
Average:		Monthly Total:			Yearly Total:		
Daily Weight							
Mon	Tues	Wed	Thurs	Fri	sat	Sun	
Morning Pulse							
Mon	Tues	Wed	Thurs	Fri	sat	Sun	

Did I meet my goals for the week? ☐ Yes   ☐ No

What helped me reach my goals or what kept me from reaching my goals:

_____

_____

How do I feel about that? _____

_____

What will I change next week? _____

What will I not change next week? _____

Notes/Other Observations: _____

_____

_____

_____

_____

*"If 15 minutes is all the time I have, I still run.
Fifteen minutes of running is better than
not running at all."*

Dr. Duncan Macdonald

Week of ___/___/_____ - ___/___/_____

Goals for Week: _____

_____

_____

MONDAY	Time	Distance	Pace	Weekly Total
Time of Day	Weather	Route/Course:		
Cross Training:				
How I Felt:				

TUESDAY	Time	Distance	Pace	Weekly Total
Time of Day	Weather	Route/Course:		
Cross Training:				
How I Felt:				

WEDNESDAY	Time	Distance	Pace	Weekly Total
Time of Day	Weather	Route/Course:		
Cross Training:				
How I Felt:				

	Time	Distance	Pace	Weekly Total
THURSDAY				

Time of Day	Weather	Route/Course:
Cross Training:		
How I Felt:		

	Time	Distance	Pace	Weekly Total
FRIDAY				

Time of Day	Weather	Route/Course:
Cross Training:		
How I Felt:		

	Time	Distance	Pace	Weekly Total
SATURDAY				

Time of Day	Weather	Route/Course:
Cross Training:		
How I Felt:		

	Time	Distance	Pace	Weekly Total
SUNDAY				

Time of Day	Weather	Route/Course:
Cross Training:		
How I Felt:		

Week 43 Wrap Up

WEEKLY SUMMARY						
Week Total:		Longest Run:			Shortest Run:	
Average:		Monthly Total:			Yearly Total:	
Daily Weight						
Mon	Tues	Wed	Thurs	Fri	sat	Sun
Morning Pulse						
Mon	Tues	Wed	Thurs	Fri	sat	Sun

Did I meet my goals for the week?   ☐ Yes   ☐ No

What helped me reach my goals or what kept me from reaching my goals:

_____

_____

How do I feel about that? _____

_____

What will I change next week? _____

What will I not change next week? _____

Notes/Other Observations: _____

_____

_____

_____

_____

_____

"In training, don't be afraid to be an oddball, eccentric, or extremist. Only by daring to go against tradition can new ways of training be learned. The trick is recognizing quickly when a new approach is counterproductive."

Benji Durden

Week of ___/___/_____ - ___/___/_____

Goals for Week: _____

_____

_____

MONDAY	Time	Distance	Pace	Weekly Total
Time of Day	Weather	Route/Course:		
Cross Training:				
How I Felt:				

TUESDAY	Time	Distance	Pace	Weekly Total
Time of Day	Weather	Route/Course:		
Cross Training:				
How I Felt:				

WEDNESDAY	Time	Distance	Pace	Weekly Total
Time of Day	Weather	Route/Course:		
Cross Training:				
How I Felt:				

THURSDAY	Time	Distance	Pace	Weekly Total
Time of Day	Weather	Route/Course:		
Cross Training:				
How I Felt:				

FRIDAY	Time	Distance	Pace	Weekly Total
Time of Day	Weather	Route/Course:		
Cross Training:				
How I Felt:				

SATURDAY	Time	Distance	Pace	Weekly Total
Time of Day	Weather	Route/Course:		
Cross Training:				
How I Felt:				

SUNDAY	Time	Distance	Pace	Weekly Total
Time of Day	Weather	Route/Course:		
Cross Training:				
How I Felt:				

Week 44 Wrap Up

WEEKLY SUMMARY						
Week Total:		Longest Run:			Shortest Run:	
Average:		Monthly Total:			Yearly Total:	
Daily Weight						
Mon	Tues	Wed	Thurs	Fri	sat	Sun
Morning Pulse						
Mon	Tues	Wed	Thurs	Fri	sat	Sun

Did I meet my goals for the week? ☐ Yes ☐ No

What helped me reach my goals or what kept me from reaching my goals:

_____

_____

How do I feel about that? _____

_____

What will I change next week? _____

What will I not change next week? _____

Notes/Other Observations: _____

_____

_____

_____

_____

> *"If ever I should forget who I am, and what I believe,
> I only need to run that path, and in my running,
> I will find my way back to myself, and
> discover once again who I am."*
>
> **Jeffrey Horowitz**

Week of ___/___/_____ - ___/___/_____

Goals for Week: _____

_____

_____

MONDAY	Time	Distance	Pace	Weekly Total
Time of Day	Weather	Route/Course:		
Cross Training:				
How I Felt:				

TUESDAY	Time	Distance	Pace	Weekly Total
Time of Day	Weather	Route/Course:		
Cross Training:				
How I Felt:				

WEDNESDAY	Time	Distance	Pace	Weekly Total
Time of Day	Weather	Route/Course:		
Cross Training:				
How I Felt:				

THURSDAY	Time	Distance	Pace	Weekly Total

Time of Day	Weather	Route/Course:

Cross Training:

How I Felt:

FRIDAY	Time	Distance	Pace	Weekly Total

Time of Day	Weather	Route/Course:

Cross Training:

How I Felt:

SATURDAY	Time	Distance	Pace	Weekly Total

Time of Day	Weather	Route/Course:

Cross Training:

How I Felt:

SUNDAY	Time	Distance	Pace	Weekly Total

Time of Day	Weather	Route/Course:

Cross Training:

How I Felt:

Week 45 Wrap Up

WEEKLY SUMMARY		
Week Total:	Longest Run:	Shortest Run:
Average:	Monthly Total:	Yearly Total:

Daily Weight						
Mon	Tues	Wed	Thurs	Fri	sat	Sun

Morning Pulse						
Mon	Tues	Wed	Thurs	Fri	sat	Sun

Did I meet my goals for the week?   ☐ Yes   ☐ No

What helped me reach my goals or what kept me from reaching my goals:

_____

_____

How do I feel about that? _____

_____

What will I change next week? _____

What will I not change next week? _____

Notes/Other Observations: _____

_____

_____

_____

_____

_____

"To be effective over the last 6 miles of a marathon, one must harbor some sort of emotional as well as physical reserves."

Kenny Moore

Week of ___/___/_____ - ___/___/_____

Goals for Week: _____

_____

_____

MONDAY	Time	Distance	Pace	Weekly Total
Time of Day	Weather	Route/Course:		
Cross Training:				
How I Felt:				

TUESDAY	Time	Distance	Pace	Weekly Total
Time of Day	Weather	Route/Course:		
Cross Training:				
How I Felt:				

WEDNESDAY	Time	Distance	Pace	Weekly Total
Time of Day	Weather	Route/Course:		
Cross Training:				
How I Felt:				

	Time	Distance	Pace	Weekly Total
THURSDAY				

Time of Day	Weather	Route/Course:

Cross Training:
How I Felt:

	Time	Distance	Pace	Weekly Total
FRIDAY				

Time of Day	Weather	Route/Course:

Cross Training:
How I Felt:

	Time	Distance	Pace	Weekly Total
SATURDAY				

Time of Day	Weather	Route/Course:

Cross Training:
How I Felt:

	Time	Distance	Pace	Weekly Total
SUNDAY				

Time of Day	Weather	Route/Course:

Cross Training:
How I Felt:

Week 46 Wrap Up

WEEKLY SUMMARY						
Week Total:		Longest Run:			Shortest Run:	
Average:		Monthly Total:			Yearly Total:	
Daily Weight						
Mon	Tues	Wed	Thurs	Fri	sat	Sun
Morning Pulse						
Mon	Tues	Wed	Thurs	Fri	sat	Sun

Did I meet my goals for the week?   ☐ Yes   ☐ No

What helped me reach my goals or what kept me from reaching my goals:

_____

_____

How do I feel about that? _____

_____

What will I change next week? _____

What will I not change next week? _____

Notes/Other Observations: _____

_____

_____

_____

_____

"When running, let your jaw hang loose, don't bunch up your shoulders close to your ears, and occasionally shake out your hands and arms to stay relaxed."

Dave Martin, Ph.D.

Week of ___/___/_____ - ___/___/_____

Goals for Week: _____

_____

_____

MONDAY	Time	Distance	Pace	Weekly Total
Time of Day	Weather	Route/Course:		
Cross Training:				
How I Felt:				

TUESDAY	Time	Distance	Pace	Weekly Total
Time of Day	Weather	Route/Course:		
Cross Training:				
How I Felt:				

WEDNESDAY	Time	Distance	Pace	Weekly Total
Time of Day	Weather	Route/Course:		
Cross Training:				
How I Felt:				

THURSDAY	Time	Distance	Pace	Weekly Total

Time of Day	Weather	Route/Course:

Cross Training:

How I Felt:

FRIDAY	Time	Distance	Pace	Weekly Total

Time of Day	Weather	Route/Course:

Cross Training:

How I Felt:

SATURDAY	Time	Distance	Pace	Weekly Total

Time of Day	Weather	Route/Course:

Cross Training:

How I Felt:

SUNDAY	Time	Distance	Pace	Weekly Total

Time of Day	Weather	Route/Course:

Cross Training:

How I Felt:

Week 47 Wrap Up

WEEKLY SUMMARY						
Week Total:		Longest Run:			Shortest Run:	
Average:		Monthly Total:			Yearly Total:	
Daily Weight						
Mon	Tues	Wed	Thurs	Fri	sat	Sun
Morning Pulse						
Mon	Tues	Wed	Thurs	Fri	sat	Sun

Did I meet my goals for the week?   ☐ Yes   ☐ No

What helped me reach my goals or what kept me from reaching my goals:

_____

_____

How do I feel about that? _____

_____

What will I change next week? _____

What will I not change next week? _____

Notes/Other Observations: _____

_____

_____

_____

_____

_____

"What distinguishes those of us at the starting line from those of us on the couch is that we learn through running to take what the days gives us, what our body will allow us, and what our will can tolerate."

John Bingham

Week of ___/___/_____ - ___/___/_____

Goals for Week: _____

_____

_____

MONDAY	Time	Distance	Pace	Weekly Total
Time of Day	Weather	Route/Course:		
Cross Training:				
How I Felt:				

TUESDAY	Time	Distance	Pace	Weekly Total
Time of Day	Weather	Route/Course:		
Cross Training:				
How I Felt:				

WEDNESDAY	Time	Distance	Pace	Weekly Total
Time of Day	Weather	Route/Course:		
Cross Training:				
How I Felt:				

THURSDAY	Time	Distance	Pace	Weekly Total
Time of Day	Weather	Route/Course:		
Cross Training:				
How I Felt:				

FRIDAY	Time	Distance	Pace	Weekly Total
Time of Day	Weather	Route/Course:		
Cross Training:				
How I Felt:				

SATURDAY	Time	Distance	Pace	Weekly Total
Time of Day	Weather	Route/Course:		
Cross Training:				
How I Felt:				

SUNDAY	Time	Distance	Pace	Weekly Total
Time of Day	Weather	Route/Course:		
Cross Training:				
How I Felt:				

Week 49 Wrap Up

WEEKLY SUMMARY				
Week Total:		Longest Run:		Shortest Run:
Average:		Monthly Total:		Yearly Total:
Daily Weight				
Mon	Tues	Wed	Thurs	Fri	sat	Sun
Morning Pulse				
Mon	Tues	Wed	Thurs	Fri	sat	Sun

Did I meet my goals for the week?   ☐ Yes   ☐ No

What helped me reach my goals or what kept me from reaching my goals:

_____

_____

How do I feel about that? _____

_____

What will I change next week? _____

What will I not change next week? _____

Notes/Other Observations: _____

_____

_____

_____

_____

_____

> *"On days you don't feel like running at all, tell yourself you are just going to jog around the block. Then go do it. Nine times out of 10, those few minutes of movement will be enough to kick you into gear, and you will want to keep going. And that one time out of 10? Hey, at least you've run one block. Which is one block more than most folks will run that day."*
>
> **Mark Remy**

Week of ___/___/_____ - ___/___/_____

Goals for Week: _____

_____

_____

MONDAY	Time	Distance	Pace	Weekly Total
Time of Day	Weather	Route/Course:		
Cross Training:				
How I Felt:				

TUESDAY	Time	Distance	Pace	Weekly Total
Time of Day	Weather	Route/Course:		
Cross Training:				
How I Felt:				

WEDNESDAY	Time	Distance	Pace	Weekly Total
Time of Day	Weather	Route/Course:		
Cross Training:				
How I Felt:				

THURSDAY	Time	Distance	Pace	Weekly Total

Time of Day	Weather	Route/Course:

Cross Training:

How I Felt:

FRIDAY	Time	Distance	Pace	Weekly Total

Time of Day	Weather	Route/Course:

Cross Training:

How I Felt:

SATURDAY	Time	Distance	Pace	Weekly Total

Time of Day	Weather	Route/Course:

Cross Training:

How I Felt:

SUNDAY	Time	Distance	Pace	Weekly Total

Time of Day	Weather	Route/Course:

Cross Training:

How I Felt:

Week 49 Wrap Up

WEEKLY SUMMARY					
Week Total:		Longest Run:			Shortest Run:
Average:		Monthly Total:			Yearly Total:
Daily Weight					
Mon	Tues	Wed	Thurs	Fri	sat	Sun
Morning Pulse					
Mon	Tues	Wed	Thurs	Fri	sat	Sun

Did I meet my goals for the week?   ☐ Yes   ☐ No

What helped me reach my goals or what kept me from reaching my goals:

_____

_____

How do I feel about that? _____

_____

What will I change next week? _____

What will I not change next week? _____

Notes/Other Observations: _____

_____

_____

_____

_____

_____

Time to Order a New Training Log.

> *"Think chest/hips/push, or CHP, when it's time for uphill running. Chest up, hips forward, push strongly off each foot."*
>
> **Jeff Galloway**

Week of ___/___/_____ - ___/___/_____

Goals for Week: _____

_____

_____

MONDAY	Time	Distance	Pace	Weekly Total
Time of Day	Weather	Route/Course:		
Cross Training:				
How I Felt:				

TUESDAY	Time	Distance	Pace	Weekly Total
Time of Day	Weather	Route/Course:		
Cross Training:				
How I Felt:				

WEDNESDAY	Time	Distance	Pace	Weekly Total
Time of Day	Weather	Route/Course:		
Cross Training:				
How I Felt:				

THURSDAY	Time	Distance	Pace	Weekly Total
Time of Day	Weather	Route/Course:		
Cross Training:				
How I Felt:				

FRIDAY	Time	Distance	Pace	Weekly Total
Time of Day	Weather	Route/Course:		
Cross Training:				
How I Felt:				

SATURDAY	Time	Distance	Pace	Weekly Total
Time of Day	Weather	Route/Course:		
Cross Training:				
How I Felt:				

SUNDAY	Time	Distance	Pace	Weekly Total
Time of Day	Weather	Route/Course:		
Cross Training:				
How I Felt:				

Week 50 Wrap Up

WEEKLY SUMMARY		
Week Total:	Longest Run:	Shortest Run:
Average:	Monthly Total:	Yearly Total:
Daily Weight						
Mon	Tues	Wed	Thurs	Fri	sat	Sun
Morning Pulse						
Mon	Tues	Wed	Thurs	Fri	sat	Sun

Did I meet my goals for the week?   ☐ Yes   ☐ No

What helped me reach my goals or what kept me from reaching my goals:

_____

_____

How do I feel about that? _____

_____

What will I change next week? _____

What will I not change next week? _____

Notes/Other Observations: _____

_____

_____

_____

_____

> *"If you have a bad workout or run a bad race, allow yourself exactly 1 hour to stew about it – then move on."*
>
> **Steve Scott**

Week of ___/___/_____ - ___/___/_____

Goals for Week: _____

_____

_____

MONDAY	Time	Distance	Pace	Weekly Total
Time of Day	Weather	Route/Course:		
Cross Training:				
How I Felt:				

TUESDAY	Time	Distance	Pace	Weekly Total
Time of Day	Weather	Route/Course:		
Cross Training:				
How I Felt:				

WEDNESDAY	Time	Distance	Pace	Weekly Total
Time of Day	Weather	Route/Course:		
Cross Training:				
How I Felt:				

THURSDAY	Time	Distance	Pace	Weekly Total

Time of Day	Weather	Route/Course:

Cross Training:

How I Felt:

FRIDAY	Time	Distance	Pace	Weekly Total

Time of Day	Weather	Route/Course:

Cross Training:

How I Felt:

SATURDAY	Time	Distance	Pace	Weekly Total

Time of Day	Weather	Route/Course:

Cross Training:

How I Felt:

SUNDAY	Time	Distance	Pace	Weekly Total

Time of Day	Weather	Route/Course:

Cross Training:

How I Felt:

Week 51 Wrap Up

WEEKLY SUMMARY						
Week Total:		Longest Run:			Shortest Run:	
Average:		Monthly Total:			Yearly Total:	
Daily Weight						
Mon	Tues	Wed	Thurs	Fri	sat	Sun
Morning Pulse						
Mon	Tues	Wed	Thurs	Fri	sat	Sun

Did I meet my goals for the week?   ☐ Yes   ☐ No

What helped me reach my goals or what kept me from reaching my goals:

_____

_____

How do I feel about that? _____

_____

What will I change next week? _____

What will I not change next week? _____

Notes/Other Observations: _____

_____

_____

_____

_____

> *"I always loved running... it was something you could do by yourself, and under your own power. You could go in any direction, fast or slow as you wanted, fighting the wind if you felt like it, seeking out new sights just on the strength of your feet and the courage of your lungs."*
>
> **Paula Radcliffe**

Week of ___/___/_____ - ___/___/_____

Goals for Week: _____

_____

_____

	Time	Distance	Pace	Weekly Total
MONDAY				
Time of Day	Weather	Route/Course:		
Cross Training:				
How I Felt:				

	Time	Distance	Pace	Weekly Total
TUESDAY				
Time of Day	Weather	Route/Course:		
Cross Training:				
How I Felt:				

	Time	Distance	Pace	Weekly Total
WEDNESDAY				
Time of Day	Weather	Route/Course:		
Cross Training:				
How I Felt:				

THURSDAY	Time	Distance	Pace	Weekly Total

Time of Day	Weather	Route/Course:

Cross Training:
How I Felt:

FRIDAY	Time	Distance	Pace	Weekly Total

Time of Day	Weather	Route/Course:

Cross Training:
How I Felt:

SATURDAY	Time	Distance	Pace	Weekly Total

Time of Day	Weather	Route/Course:

Cross Training:
How I Felt:

SUNDAY	Time	Distance	Pace	Weekly Total

Time of Day	Weather	Route/Course:

Cross Training:
How I Felt:

Week 52 Wrap Up

WEEKLY SUMMARY							
Week Total:		Longest Run:			Shortest Run:		
Average:		Monthly Total:			Yearly Total:		
Daily Weight							
Mon	Tues	Wed	Thurs		Fri	sat	Sun
Morning Pulse							
Mon	Tues	Wed	Thurs		Fri	sat	Sun

Did I meet my goals for the week?   ☐ Yes   ☐ No

What helped me reach my goals or what kept me from reaching my goals:

_____

_____

How do I feel about that? _____

_____

What will I change next week? _____

What will I not change next week? _____

Notes/Other Observations: _____

_____

_____

_____

_____

_____

Congratulations! You've Completed the Year. Time to Break In a New Running Log with New Goals and New Achievements.

"You are truly your own hero in running. It is up to you to have the responsibility and self-discipline to get the job done."

Adam Goucher

Race Logs

Keep a record of the races in which you participate. Not only is it a fun habit to get into so you can refresh your memories of your race history and accomplishments, but also, it's a good measurement of performance that will help you spot trends, learn from your weak performances and build on your strong ones.

NOTE: in the Notes/Other Observations area, consider including your pace. And if you took splits during the race, consider recording those, too.

"The difference between a jogger and a runner is a race-entry blank."

Dr. George Sheehan

"You're running on guts. On fumes. Your muscles twitch. You throw up. You're delirious. But you keep running because there's no way out of this hell you're in, because there's no way you're not crossing the finish line. It's a misery that non-runners don't understand."

Martine Costello

"To me, the real test of one's character isn't defined by completing the marathon on race day, but rather by having the self-discipline and dedication to commit, sacrifice, and endure the months of training required to complete such an event."

Kimberly Pasienza

Race Log

Race Name: _____

Distance: _____ My Personal Best at this Distance: _____

Run in this Race Before? ☐ Yes   ☐ No

If "Yes", What Was My Time: _____

Running   ☐ Alone   ☐ with Friends

Friends Participating: _____

_____

Attitude at Beginning of Race: _____

_____

Attitude at End of Race: _____

_____

Time: _____ Overall Place: _____ Age Division Place: _____

Best Thing about this Race: _____

Worst Thing about this Race: _____

Would I Run this Race Again? ☐ Yes   ☐ No

Why or Why Not? _____

_____

Notes/Other Observations: _____

_____

_____

_____

Race Log

Race Name: _____

Distance: _____ My Personal Best at this Distance: _____

Run in this Race Before? ☐ Yes   ☐ No

If "Yes", What Was My Time: _____

Running ☐ Alone   ☐ with Friends

Friends Participating: _____

_____

Attitude at Beginning of Race: _____

_____

Attitude at End of Race: _____

_____

Time: _____ Overall Place: _____ Age Division Place: _____

Best Thing about this Race: _____

Worst Thing about this Race: _____

Would I Run this Race Again? ☐ Yes   ☐ No

Why or Why Not? _____

_____

Notes/Other Observations: _____

_____

_____

_____

Race Log

Race Name: _____

Distance: _____ My Personal Best at this Distance: _____

Run in this Race Before? ☐ Yes   ☐ No

If "Yes", What Was My Time: _____

Running   ☐ Alone   ☐ with Friends

Friends Participating: _____
_____

Attitude at Beginning of Race: _____
_____

Attitude at End of Race: _____
_____

Time: _____ Overall Place: _____ Age Division Place: _____

Best Thing about this Race: _____

Worst Thing about this Race: _____

Would I Run this Race Again? ☐ Yes   ☐ No

Why or Why Not? _____
_____

Notes/Other Observations: _____
_____
_____
_____

Race Log

Race Name: _____

Distance: _____ My Personal Best at this Distance: _____

Run in this Race Before? ☐ Yes   ☐ No

If "Yes", What Was My Time: _____

Running   ☐ Alone   ☐ with Friends

Friends Participating: _____

_____

Attitude at Beginning of Race: _____

_____

Attitude at End of Race: _____

_____

Time: _____ Overall Place: _____ Age Division Place: _____

Best Thing about this Race: _____

Worst Thing about this Race: _____

Would I Run this Race Again? ☐ Yes   ☐ No

Why or Why Not? _____

_____

Notes/Other Observations: _____

_____

_____

_____

Race Log

Race Name: _____

Distance: _____ My Personal Best at this Distance: _____

Run in this Race Before? ☐ Yes   ☐ No

If "Yes", What Was My Time: _____

Running ☐ Alone   ☐ with Friends

Friends Participating: _____

_____

Attitude at Beginning of Race: _____

_____

Attitude at End of Race: _____

_____

Time: _____ Overall Place: _____ Age Division Place: _____

Best Thing about this Race: _____

Worst Thing about this Race: _____

Would I Run this Race Again? ☐ Yes   ☐ No

Why or Why Not? _____

_____

Notes/Other Observations: _____

_____

_____

_____

Race Log

Race Name: _____

Distance: _____ My Personal Best at this Distance: _____

Run in this Race Before? ☐ Yes   ☐ No

If "Yes", What Was My Time: _____

Running ☐ Alone   ☐ with Friends

Friends Participating: _____

_____

Attitude at Beginning of Race: _____

_____

Attitude at End of Race: _____

_____

Time: _____ Overall Place: _____ Age Division Place: _____

Best Thing about this Race: _____

Worst Thing about this Race: _____

Would I Run this Race Again? ☐ Yes   ☐ No

Why or Why Not? _____

_____

Notes/Other Observations: _____

_____

_____

_____

Race Log

Race Name: _____

Distance: _____ My Personal Best at this Distance: _____

Run in this Race Before? ☐ Yes   ☐ No

If "Yes", What Was My Time: _____

Running   ☐ Alone   ☐ with Friends

Friends Participating: _____

_____

Attitude at Beginning of Race: _____

_____

Attitude at End of Race: _____

_____

Time: _____ Overall Place: _____ Age Division Place: _____

Best Thing about this Race: _____

Worst Thing about this Race: _____

Would I Run this Race Again? ☐ Yes   ☐ No

Why or Why Not? _____

_____

Notes/Other Observations: _____

_____

_____

_____

Race Log

Race Name: _____

Distance: _____ My Personal Best at this Distance: _____

Run in this Race Before? ☐ Yes ☐ No

If "Yes", What Was My Time: _____

Running ☐ Alone ☐ with Friends

Friends Participating: _____

_____

Attitude at Beginning of Race: _____

_____

Attitude at End of Race: _____

_____

Time: _____ Overall Place: _____ Age Division Place: _____

Best Thing about this Race: _____

Worst Thing about this Race: _____

Would I Run this Race Again? ☐ Yes ☐ No

Why or Why Not? _____

_____

Notes/Other Observations: _____

_____

_____

_____

Race Log

Race Name: _____

Distance: _____ My Personal Best at this Distance: _____

Run in this Race Before? ☐ Yes   ☐ No

If "Yes", What Was My Time: _____

Running   ☐ Alone   ☐ with Friends

Friends Participating: _____

_____

Attitude at Beginning of Race: _____

_____

Attitude at End of Race: _____

_____

Time: _____ Overall Place: _____ Age Division Place: _____

Best Thing about this Race: _____

Worst Thing about this Race: _____

Would I Run this Race Again? ☐ Yes   ☐ No

Why or Why Not? _____

_____

Notes/Other Observations: _____

_____

_____

_____

Race Log

Race Name: _____

Distance: _____ My Personal Best at this Distance: _____

Run in this Race Before? ☐ Yes   ☐ No

If "Yes", What Was My Time: _____

Running   ☐ Alone   ☐ with Friends

Friends Participating: _____

_____

Attitude at Beginning of Race: _____

_____

Attitude at End of Race: _____

_____

Time: _____ Overall Place: _____ Age Division Place: _____

Best Thing about this Race: _____

Worst Thing about this Race: _____

Would I Run this Race Again? ☐ Yes   ☐ No

Why or Why Not? _____

_____

Notes/Other Observations: _____

_____

_____

_____

Race Log

Race Name: _____

Distance: _____ My Personal Best at this Distance: _____

Run in this Race Before? ☐ Yes   ☐ No

If "Yes", What Was My Time: _____

Running ☐ Alone   ☐ with Friends

Friends Participating: _____
_____

Attitude at Beginning of Race: _____
_____

Attitude at End of Race: _____
_____

Time: _____ Overall Place: _____ Age Division Place: _____

Best Thing about this Race: _____

Worst Thing about this Race: _____

Would I Run this Race Again? ☐ Yes   ☐ No

Why or Why Not? _____
_____

Notes/Other Observations: _____
_____
_____
_____

Race Log

Race Name: _____

Distance: _____ My Personal Best at this Distance: _____

Run in this Race Before? ☐ Yes   ☐ No

If "Yes", What Was My Time: _____

Running   ☐ Alone   ☐ with Friends

Friends Participating: _____

_____

Attitude at Beginning of Race: _____

_____

Attitude at End of Race: _____

_____

Time: _____ Overall Place: _____ Age Division Place: _____

Best Thing about this Race: _____

Worst Thing about this Race: _____

Would I Run this Race Again? ☐ Yes   ☐ No

Why or Why Not? _____

_____

Notes/Other Observations: _____

_____

_____

_____

Race Log

Race Name: _____

Distance: _____ My Personal Best at this Distance: _____

Run in this Race Before? ☐ Yes   ☐ No

If "Yes", What Was My Time: _____

Running ☐ Alone   ☐ with Friends

Friends Participating: _____

_____

Attitude at Beginning of Race: _____

_____

Attitude at End of Race: _____

_____

Time: _____ Overall Place: _____ Age Division Place: _____

Best Thing about this Race: _____

Worst Thing about this Race: _____

Would I Run this Race Again? ☐ Yes   ☐ No

Why or Why Not? _____

_____

Notes/Other Observations: _____

_____

_____

_____

Race Log

Race Name: _____

Distance: _____ My Personal Best at this Distance: _____

Run in this Race Before? ☐ Yes   ☐ No

If "Yes", What Was My Time: _____

Running   ☐ Alone   ☐ with Friends

Friends Participating: _____

_____

Attitude at Beginning of Race: _____

_____

Attitude at End of Race: _____

_____

Time: _____   Overall Place: _____   Age Division Place: _____

Best Thing about this Race: _____

Worst Thing about this Race: _____

Would I Run this Race Again?   ☐ Yes   ☐ No

Why or Why Not? _____

_____

Notes/Other Observations: _____

_____

_____

_____

Race Log

Race Name: _____

Distance: _____ My Personal Best at this Distance: _____

Run in this Race Before? ☐ Yes   ☐ No

If "Yes", What Was My Time: _____

Running ☐ Alone   ☐ with Friends

Friends Participating: _____

_____

Attitude at Beginning of Race: _____

_____

Attitude at End of Race: _____

_____

Time: _____ Overall Place: _____ Age Division Place: _____

Best Thing about this Race: _____

Worst Thing about this Race: _____

Would I Run this Race Again? ☐ Yes   ☐ No

Why or Why Not? _____

_____

Notes/Other Observations: _____

_____

_____

_____

Race Log

Race Name: _____

Distance: _____ My Personal Best at this Distance: _____

Run in this Race Before? ☐ Yes   ☐ No

If "Yes", What Was My Time: _____

Running ☐ Alone   ☐ with Friends

Friends Participating: _____
_____

Attitude at Beginning of Race: _____
_____

Attitude at End of Race: _____
_____

Time: _____ Overall Place: _____ Age Division Place: _____

Best Thing about this Race: _____

Worst Thing about this Race: _____

Would I Run this Race Again? ☐ Yes   ☐ No

Why or Why Not? _____
_____

Notes/Other Observations: _____
_____
_____
_____

Race Log

Race Name: _____

Distance: _____ My Personal Best at this Distance: _____

Run in this Race Before? ☐ Yes   ☐ No

If "Yes", What Was My Time: _____

Running ☐ Alone   ☐ with Friends

Friends Participating: _____

_____

Attitude at Beginning of Race: _____

_____

Attitude at End of Race: _____

_____

Time: _____ Overall Place: _____ Age Division Place: _____

Best Thing about this Race: _____

Worst Thing about this Race: _____

Would I Run this Race Again? ☐ Yes   ☐ No

Why or Why Not? _____

_____

Notes/Other Observations: _____

_____

_____

_____

Race Log

Race Name: _____

Distance: _____ My Personal Best at this Distance: _____

Run in this Race Before? ☐ Yes   ☐ No

If "Yes", What Was My Time: _____

Running ☐ Alone   ☐ with Friends

Friends Participating: _____

_____

Attitude at Beginning of Race: _____

_____

Attitude at End of Race: _____

_____

Time: _____ Overall Place: _____ Age Division Place: _____

Best Thing about this Race: _____

Worst Thing about this Race: _____

Would I Run this Race Again? ☐ Yes   ☐ No

Why or Why Not? _____

_____

Notes/Other Observations: _____

_____

_____

_____

Race Log

Race Name: _____

Distance: _____ My Personal Best at this Distance: _____

Run in this Race Before? ☐ Yes   ☐ No

If "Yes", What Was My Time: _____

Running   ☐ Alone   ☐ with Friends

Friends Participating: _____

_____

Attitude at Beginning of Race: _____

_____

Attitude at End of Race: _____

_____

Time: _____ Overall Place: _____ Age Division Place: _____

Best Thing about this Race: _____

Worst Thing about this Race: _____

Would I Run this Race Again? ☐ Yes   ☐ No

Why or Why Not? _____

_____

Notes/Other Observations: _____

_____

_____

_____

Race Log

Race Name: _____

Distance: _____ My Personal Best at this Distance: _____

Run in this Race Before? ☐ Yes   ☐ No

If "Yes", What Was My Time: _____

Running   ☐ Alone   ☐ with Friends

Friends Participating: _____

_____

Attitude at Beginning of Race: _____

_____

Attitude at End of Race: _____

_____

Time: _____   Overall Place: _____   Age Division Place: _____

Best Thing about this Race: _____

Worst Thing about this Race: _____

Would I Run this Race Again? ☐ Yes   ☐ No

Why or Why Not? _____

_____

Notes/Other Observations: _____

_____

_____

_____

Race Log

Race Name: _____

Distance: _____ My Personal Best at this Distance: _____

Run in this Race Before? ☐ Yes   ☐ No

If "Yes", What Was My Time: _____

Running ☐ Alone   ☐ with Friends

Friends Participating: _____

_____

Attitude at Beginning of Race: _____

_____

Attitude at End of Race: _____

_____

Time: _____ Overall Place: _____ Age Division Place: _____

Best Thing about this Race: _____

Worst Thing about this Race: _____

Would I Run this Race Again? ☐ Yes   ☐ No

Why or Why Not? _____

_____

Notes/Other Observations: _____

_____

_____

_____

Race Log

Race Name: _____

Distance: _____ My Personal Best at this Distance: _____

Run in this Race Before? ☐ Yes   ☐ No

If "Yes", What Was My Time: _____

Running   ☐ Alone   ☐ with Friends

Friends Participating: _____
_____

Attitude at Beginning of Race: _____
_____

Attitude at End of Race: _____
_____

Time: _____ Overall Place: _____ Age Division Place: _____

Best Thing about this Race: _____

Worst Thing about this Race: _____

Would I Run this Race Again? ☐ Yes   ☐ No

Why or Why Not? _____
_____

Notes/Other Observations: _____
_____
_____
_____

Race Log

Race Name: _____

Distance: _____ My Personal Best at this Distance: _____

Run in this Race Before? ☐ Yes   ☐ No

If "Yes", What Was My Time: _____

Running   ☐ Alone   ☐ with Friends

Friends Participating: _____

_____

Attitude at Beginning of Race: _____

_____

Attitude at End of Race: _____

_____

Time: _____ Overall Place: _____ Age Division Place: _____

Best Thing about this Race: _____

Worst Thing about this Race: _____

Would I Run this Race Again? ☐ Yes   ☐ No

Why or Why Not? _____

_____

Notes/Other Observations: _____

_____

_____

_____

Race Log

Race Name: _____

Distance: _____ My Personal Best at this Distance: _____

Run in this Race Before? ☐ Yes   ☐ No

If "Yes", What Was My Time: _____

Running   ☐ Alone   ☐ with Friends

Friends Participating: _____
_____

Attitude at Beginning of Race: _____
_____

Attitude at End of Race: _____
_____

Time: _____ Overall Place: _____ Age Division Place: _____

Best Thing about this Race: _____

Worst Thing about this Race: _____

Would I Run this Race Again? ☐ Yes   ☐ No

Why or Why Not? _____
_____

Notes/Other Observations: _____
_____
_____
_____

"Why run? I run because I am an animal. I run because it is part of my genetic wiring. I run because millions of years of evolution have left me programmed to run. And finally, I run because there's no better way to see the sun rise and set... What the years have shown me is that running clarifies the thinking process as well as purifies the body. I think best – most broadly and most fully – when I am running."

Amby Burfoot

Footwear Log

First Wear Date	Brand	Model	Size	Last Wear Date	Total Mileage
Notes:					
Notes:					
Notes:					
Notes:					
Notes:					
Notes:					
Notes:					
Notes:					

"A good pair of running shoes should last you 400 to 500 miles and is one of the most critical purchases you will make." **John Hanc**

Footwear Log

First Wear Date	Brand	Model	Size	Last Wear Date	Total Mileage
Notes:					
Notes:					
Notes:					
Notes:					
Notes:					
Notes:					
Notes:					
Notes:					

"I double-knot my shoe laces. It's a pain untying your shoes afterward – particularly if you get them wet -- but so is stopping in the middle of a race to tie them." **Hal Higdon**

The Perceptive Runner

Here is one of the inspirational stories from the book "Olympic Spirit" by R. Scott Frothingham, available at amazon.com and other retailers.

The Perceptive Runner

When Mongolian Pyambu Tuul started the marathon at the 1992 Barcelona Olympics, he was not expected to win a medal. And he performed as expected, falling back to the rear of the pack soon after the start of Games' most grueling event.

When Hwang Young-cho of Korea crossed after the line in 2 hours 13 minutes and 23 seconds to win the Gold medal, Tuul still was about two hours away from the stadium.

When he came in last, finishing the race a couple of minutes over four hours, a reporter asked him why he was so slow and he replied '"No, my time was not slow, after all you could call my run a Mongolian Olympic marathon record."

Then another reporter asked him whether it was the greatest day of his life and Tuul humbly offered this stunning response:

"And as for it being the greatest day of my life, no it isn't", he said, "Up till six months ago I had no sight at all. I was a totally blind person. When I trained it was only with the aid of friends who ran with me. But a group of doctors came to my country last year to do humanitarian medical work. One doctor took a look at my eyes and asked me questions. I told him I had been unable to see since childhood. He said 'But I can fix your sight with a simple operation'. So he did the operation on me and after 20 years I could see again. So today wasn't the greatest day of my life. The best day was when I got my sight back and I saw my wife and two daughters for the first time. And they are beautiful."

Recommendations

Here are 5 quotes from Olympic Medal winners (selected from the 140+ quotes in the book "Olympic Gold" available on amazon.com and from other retailers).

"The greatest memory for me of the 1984 Olympics was not the individual honors, but standing on the podium with my teammates to receive our team gold medal." - Mitch Gaylord, 4 time Olympic medalist - gymnastics

"I didn't set out to beat the world; I just set out to do my absolute best." -Al Oerter, 4 time Olympic medalist - track and field

"It is the inspiration of the Olympic Games that drives people not only to compete but to improve, and to bring lasting spiritual and moral benefits to the athlete and inspiration to those lucky enough to witness the athletic dedication." - Herb Elliott, 1 time Olympic medalist - track and field

"We all have dreams. But in order to make dreams come into reality, it takes an awful lot of determination, dedication, self-discipline, and effort." -Jesse Owens, 4 time Olympic medalist - track and field

"At the two-thirds mark, I think of those who are still with me. Who might break? Should I? Then I give it all I've got." -Ibrahim Hussein, 2 Olympic Games- track and field

Also available from amazon.com and other retailers:

> "People sometimes sneer at those who run every day,
> claiming they'll go to any length to live longer.
> But don't think that's the reason most people run.
> Most runners run not because they want to live longer,
> but because they want to live life to the fullest.
> If you're going to while away the years,
> it's far better to live them with clear goals
> and fully alive then in a fog,
> and I believe running
> helps you to do that.
> Exerting yourself to the fullest
> within your individual limits:
> that's the essence of running,
> and a metaphor for life…"
>
> **Haruki Murakami**

FRONT COVER PHOTO: hojusaram, https://www.flickr.com/photos/hojusaram/2339091527/ March 16, 2008 licensed through Creative Commons Generic (CC BY-SA 2.0) http://creativecommons.org/licenses/by-sa/2.0/legalcode

BACK COVER PHOTO: "Yellow Road Marking Sherman Tan Singapore http://www.flickr.com/photos/56502208@N00/454775320/ April 11, 2007 licensed through Creative Commons Generic (CC BY-SA 2.0) http://creativecommons.org/licenses/by-sa/2.0/legalcode

May your miles be many
and your injuries few.
Here's to PBs a plenty --
a life of amazing runs for you.

Sebastian

Copyright © 2015 FastForward Publishing All rights reserved.
Permission to reproduce or transmit in any form or by any means,
electronic or mechanical, including photocopying and recording,
or by any information storage or retrieval system, must be obtained
in writing from FastForward Publishing.

FastForwardPublishing.com

Made in United States
North Haven, CT
27 December 2021